ELEMENTS OF
ACOUSTIC PHONETICS

Andrew Linn
Cambridge 1991

ELEMENTS OF
ACOUSTIC PHONETICS

PETER LADEFOGED

THE UNIVERSITY OF CHICAGO PRESS

CHICAGO & LONDON

The University of Chicago Press, Chicago 60637
The University of Chicago Press, Ltd., London

ISBN 0-226-46784-8 (cloth); 0-226-46785-6 (paper)
LCN 62-8349

Preface

This book gives an account of some aspects of acoustics for the benefit of linguists and phoneticians. It assumes that the reader knows no physics or mathematics, but nevertheless wants to be able to follow some of the discussions of acoustic phonetics which are prevalent in the current technical journals. Consequently it tries to give him a background knowledge of such acoustics as will enable him to appreciate the general principles involved, without encumbering him with too many technicalities or with irrelevant material of the kind that is normally found in elementary physics textbooks. Thus the theory of resonance as presented here contains one or two technical inaccuracies which have been introduced in the interests of simplicity; and there is no consideration of the speed of sound, nor of the Doppler effect, nor of the properties of closed and open organ pipes, since none of these matters has a direct bearing on the acoustics of speech.

Two other limitations of the scope of this book must also be noted here. Firstly, it is intended to be a textbook explaining the preliminaries to a theory; it is not meant to be a comprehensive account of the physics of speech; indeed, it does not even attempt to survey the present state of investigations in acoustic phonetics. Secondly, it is not concerned with the use of instruments such as the sound spectrograph. The laboratory techniques for the acoustic analysis of speech are considered in the author's forthcoming introduction to experimental phonetics: *Speech in the Laboratory*. The present book covers only the preliminaries which must be understood before some of the techniques outlined therein can be properly used.

My thanks are due to many people who read a draft of this book and made helpful comments; foremost among them are: David Abercrombie, Ian Catford, Martin Joos, Jenny Ladefoged and R. Sillitoe.

Contents

Preface   v

Chapter 1. Sound Waves   1

       2. Loudness and Pitch   13

       3. Quality   22

       4. Wave Analysis   34

       5. Resonance   55

       6. Hearing   71

       7. The Production of Speech   89

Appendix 1. Glossary   109

        2. Annotated Bibliography   115

Index   119

1

Sound Waves

One of the main difficulties of studying speech is that sounds are so fleeting and transient. As each word is uttered it ceases to exist. The sounds can, it is true, be recalled, either by repeating the words, or by using recording instruments such as the gramophone. But in both these cases it is another event that is happening. It is a copy of the original sound, not the sound itself.

Even during the brief existence of a sound it is curiously difficult to examine. There is nothing that can be seen; there is no visible connecting link between a speaker and a listener. There is air around; but it is not normally possible to *see* any changes in the condition of the air when it is conveying a sound.

Because of these difficulties, it is perhaps best to begin our study of sound with a brief examination of the human ear. In this way we start with something tangible; for we know that the ear is the organ of hearing. Although there is still some uncertainty concerning the exact mechanism of the ear, we can nevertheless explain a number of facts about sound in terms of a simplified theory.

Figure 1.1 is a schematic diagram of the essential features of the ear. The first part to note is the eardrum, which is a thin membrane just over an inch down the narrow tube, or auditory passage, leading from the outer ear. When air is pushed down the auditory passage the eardrum tends to move with it; similarly it moves back as the air moves away. Connected to the eardrum is a chain of bones whose function is to transmit the movements of the eardrum to the liquid which is in the inner ear. Through the action of the bone chain the back and forth vibrations of the eardrum cause vibrations in the liquid. Closely linked with this liquid are the nerves which lead to the auditory sensation area of the brain. Movements of the liquid

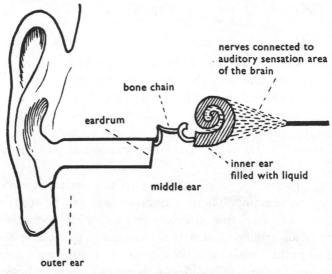

FIG. I.I. A schematic diagram of the mechanism of the ear.

stimulate these nerves so that we experience the sensation of hearing. Bringing all these facts together we may say that a sound is any disturbance of the air that could cause a displacement of the eardrum which, after transmission by the bone chain, could affect the liquid in the inner ear in such a way that the auditory nerves are stimulated. Our investigation into the nature of sound will be largely concerned with an examination of the disturbances in the air that can set off this process.

If we now turn to consider the origins of different sounds, we find that in every case some form of movement is involved. Thus a noise occurs when a falling book hits the ground; a piano and a violin have strings that vibrate; and most speech sounds are caused by a movement of air from the lungs. It is

these movements that set up the disturbances in the surrounding air.

The disturbances, however, do not occur instantaneously
throughout all the air around the source of sound. They spread
outwards like ripples on a pond, so that there must be a short
delay from the moment when the original movement caused
the first disturbance to the instant when the disturbance reaches
our ears. Sound travels very quickly, and consequently when
we watch a person talking, we seem to hear the sounds at the
same time as we see the movements that caused them. But in
fact a small time has elapsed; and, as we all know, in the case
of a distant source of sound such as a gun, the flash of the
explosion is often seen an appreciable time before the explosion
is heard.

In order to explain this phenomenon it is convenient to
think of the air between our ears and a source of sound as being
divided up into a number of particles. The source of sound
causes movements of the air particles in its immediate neigh-
bourhood; these movements cause disturbances in the air a
little farther away from the source; these air particles in their
turn affect their neighbours which are still farther away from
the source; and so the disturbance spreads outwards.

We may begin our detailed examination of the production
of sound by considering the note made by a tuning fork. If you
look carefully at a tuning fork while it is sounding you can see
that the edges of the prongs are slightly blurred, because they
are vibrating rapidly from side to side. This movement, which
has been shown in an exaggerated form in figure 1.2, makes a
series of blows on the adjacent air. The diagram represents a
moment when the right-hand prong of the fork has moved as
far as possible to the right. At that moment the particle of air
immediately alongside the fork has been moved so that it is
now closer to the neighbouring air particles. When the air
particles are close together the air is compressed; and, on the
other hand, when they are farther apart than normal there is

what is called an area of rarefaction. A moment later, as the prongs of the fork spring together again, the air will be drawn back so that there is an area of rarefaction alongside the fork.

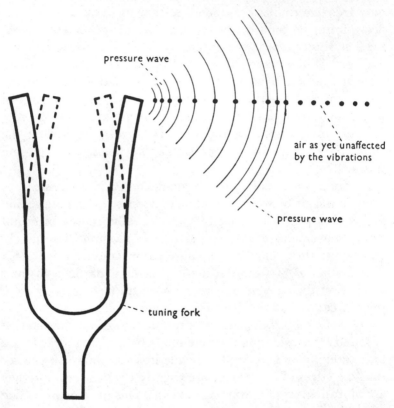

FIG. 1.2. Diagrammatic representation of fluctuations in air pressure caused by a vibrating tuning fork.

Thus, as the fork vibrates, the air alongside it will be alternately compressed and rarefied. This disturbance of the air alongside the fork will have an effect on the particles of air a little farther away. Small displacements of the air spread outwards as indicated in the diagram; when they arrive at a listener's ear they will cause the eardrum to move, and this will result in their being perceived as sound.

To get a clearer picture of the behaviour of the air we may consider the motion of a limited number of particles of air. In figure 1.3, the movements of thirteen air particles are represented (in a slightly simplified form). Each line of the diagram shows their positions a short interval of time after the moment represented in the preceding line. Line six, for instance, represents the positions these thirteen particles have assumed a moment after they were in the position indicated in line five. In this diagram stationary particles are indicated by a dash; when the particle is moving an arrow is used, the speed of movement being indicated by the boldness of the arrow. Positions of the tuning fork for corresponding times are shown on the left of the figure.

It is important to note that figure 1.3 is a kind of chart, and not, like figure 1.2, a diagrammatic picture of an event. It does not represent what happens to a whole body of air when a tuning fork sounds. Only thirteen particles are represented, the successive positions of these particles being shown in successive lines. Because each line represents a moment in time later than that of the line above, the diagram should be examined one line at a time. It is a good idea to begin by placing a sheet of paper on the diagram so that only the top line is visible. As you move the paper down the page the areas of compression and rarefaction will appear to move to the right, although the individual air particles move only backwards and forwards.

This kind of phenomenon is known as a *wave*. It is typical of a wave movement that energy in the form of areas of compression and rarefaction should be transmitted considerable distances through a medium such as the air, although the individual parts of the medium are each only slightly displaced from their positions of rest.

In order to understand exactly how a wave motion is trans-

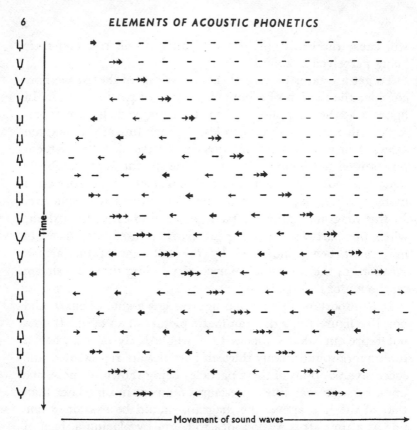

FIG. 1.3. The spreading of a sound wave. Each line shows the position of thirteen particles of air at a moment in time a little later than that in the line above. Stationary particles are indicated by a dash; moving particles are shown by arrows, the boldness of the arrow indicating the speed of movement. Highly schematised positions of a tuning fork which might have produced these movements are shown on the left. (Sophisticated readers, for whom this book is not intended, will note that the wavefront has been slightly falsified in the interests of simplicity; it is assumed that the wave starts with its maximum amplitude.)

mitted, we must make a more detailed examination of figure 1.3. When we examine the diagram line by line we see that in the first line the prongs of the tuning fork are moving rapidly outwards through their positions of rest. All the particles are stationary except the first one which is moving in sympathy with the tuning fork. In the second line, which represents the state of affairs a moment later, the first particle is slowing down slightly, since it has pushed against the second particle which is now moving rapidly. In the third line (a moment later still) the first particle has come to rest, and the second particle is slowing down, having set the third particle in motion. In the fourth line the third particle is still moving outwards, and has even set the fourth particle in motion. The second particle however has stopped, and the first particle is moving back towards the tuning fork, the prongs of which are now moving towards one another. Each air particle is behaving like the bob of a pendulum. If you give a pendulum a push so that it moves to one side it will move a certain distance, and then start swinging back through its position of rest; similarly each air particle is like a pendulum which has received its push from the particle next to it. Particle seven is set in motion by particle six, which in its turn owes its movement to the push given to it by particle five, and so on.

It is in this way that vibratory motion is transmitted through the air. The individual particles move backwards and forwards, whilst the waves of compression move steadily outwards. Consequently a listening ear will experience moments of higher pressure followed by moments of lower pressure. This will affect the eardrum in the way we have already mentioned, so that the sensation of sound results.

Not all variations in air pressure are perceivable as sounds. For example we can produce by means of a fan a movement of air accompanied by a pressure wave that can be felt but not heard. In this case there is definitely a disturbance of the air; but this kind of variation in air pressure cannot be sensed by the ear because only very rapid fluctuations of air pressure affect the ear in such a way that sounds are perceived.

Anything which causes an appropriate variation in air

pressure is a source of sound. As we have seen, the changes in air pressure are due to small but frequent movements of the air particles. These have arisen because the source of sound is making similar movements. Usually the movements are far too fast to be seen with the eye. But if you put your finger lightly against a sounding tuning fork, you can often feel the vibrations. The pressure of your finger will probably stop the movement, and hence the sound will cease. In the same way a ringing glass can be stilled by placing a hand upon it, and thus stopping the glass vibrating. Both a glass and a tuning fork are sources of sound only as long as they are vibrating.

Another comparatively simple source of sound is a stretched string. When this is plucked or pushed to one side and then released, it springs back through and beyond its original position, and starts vibrating. This is the basis of musical instruments such as the harp, guitar, and violin. A piano also uses stretched strings, or wires, but in this case they are hit with small hammers, instead of being plucked or bowed to one side.

Some sources of sound do not cause such regular vibrations of the air. When a falling book hits the ground there is a noise although there is nothing like a stretched string or a tuning fork vibrating. The sound is caused partly by the sudden compression of the air beneath the book, and partly by the diverse irregular movements set up in both the book and the floor.

The source of sound with which we are most concerned is the human voice. Here fluctuations in air pressure are caused by a variety of means. The most important of these is the rapid opening and closing of the vocal cords. Each time the vocal cords are closed pressure is built up, which is suddenly released when they are opened. Consequently the rapid opening and closing of the cords causes a series of sharp variations in air pressure. As we shall see later (Chapter 7) these variations in air pressure affect the air in the throat and mouth in such a way that speech sound is produced.

Diagrams

In our discussions of sounds it will be useful to have some means of representing them as visible shapes. This necessity leads us to a short consideration of the principles of drawing diagrams. So far we have been describing sounds in terms of the movements of the air particles, and also in terms of variations in air pressure. Our problem is to represent these movements and pressures in a suitable way.

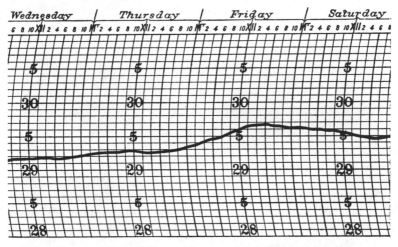

FIG. 1.4. An example of a barograph record, showing day by day variations in the pressure of the atmosphere.

One well known method of recording air pressures is by means of a barometer. It is, of course, unsuitable for measuring the minute and rapid variations in air pressure which are associated with sounds. But it does give us an indication of the kind of diagram we might be able to produce. A barograph, which is a kind of barometer with its pointer in contact with a sheet of paper on a slowly revolving drum, will produce a record as shown in figure 1.4. Here the variations in air pressure are shown in one direction, and the times at which they occur in the other. Similarly, with the aid of a microphone—

an instrument which is electrically sensitive to small variations in air pressure—combined with other electrical recording devices, we can produce a graph (figure 1.5) of the variations

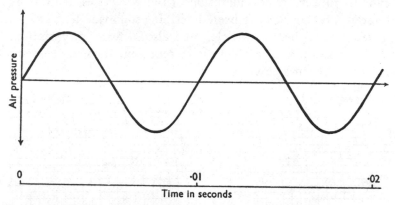

FIG. 1.5. The variations in air pressure during the sounding of a tuning fork.

in air pressure which occur during the sounding of a tuning fork. In this case the changes in pressure occur at very great speeds. The pressure rises smoothly to a maximum, and then falls away steadily to a minimum before rising again to repeat the cycle, all within a small fraction of a second. The height of any point on the curve above the centre line represents the increase of air pressure at that time. Points below the line indicate air pressures below the normal level of the surrounding air.

From a diagram such as figure 1.5 we can see firstly the extent of the maximum increase of air pressure, secondly the rate at which maximum peaks of pressure occur (in this case one every one hundredth of a second), and thirdly the way in which the pressure builds up and then decays. As these are the most important aspects of a sound wave, figure 1.5 is a useful form of diagram of a sound.

The variations in air pressure are directly related to the

movements of the air particles. Peaks of pressure occur when they are close together, and moments of low pressure when they are furthest apart. Another way of representing a sound is to diagram these movements of air particles. As we stated earlier, the movement of the top of one of the prongs of a tuning fork corresponds to that of the neighbouring air particles. Now it is fairly easy to make the movement of a tuning fork visible by attaching a sharp point to one prong and then drawing the vibrating fork over a sheet of paper at an even rate (figure 1.6).

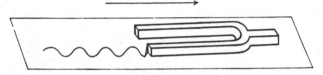

FIG. 1.6. A tuning fork being moved over a sheet of paper showing the vibrations of one of the prongs (much exaggerated).

A more practical method of carrying out this experiment is to allow the vibrating fork to remain stationary above a sheet of smoked paper wrapped round a drum which revolves at a constant speed. But in either case a curve of the form shown results.

If we now look again at figure 1.3 we can see how a curve of a similar shape can be built up from a consideration of the movement of an air particle. In figure 1.3 the position of each particle is shown at regular intervals of time. Consequently a curve drawn through the positions of any one particle will show how much it has been displaced from its position of rest at any particular time. This is one of the most common methods of representing a sound. An example using the arrows of figure 1.3, but with the time scale shown horizontally, is given in figure 1.7. When the curve is above the line it means that the particle, at that time, is displaced from its position of rest away from the source of sound (i.e. to the right in figure 1.3);

when the curve is below the line it means that the particle is displaced towards the source (i.e. to the left). We should also note that the particles are stationary for a brief instant at the point of their maximum displacement; and that they are moving at their fastest as they pass their original position.

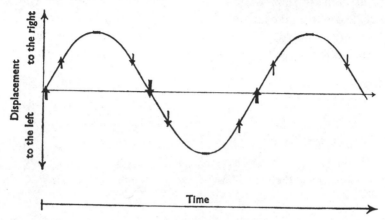

FIG. 1.7. The movement of an air particle during the sounding of a tuning fork.

Generally speaking, in this book we shall be considering sounds as variations in air pressure. Consequently the most useful form of diagram will be one which shows how the air pressure at a given place varies over a period of time (as in figure 1.5). We must remember, however, that it is also possible to draw a diagram of the same phenomena by showing the movement of an individual air particle (as in figure 1.7). These two forms of diagram are simply different ways of looking at the same event.

2

Loudness and Pitch

If you listen to a number of musical notes, such as those made by tuning forks, pianos, or violins, you will find that they may differ from one another in three principal ways. Firstly, one may be louder than another; if you strike two similar tuning forks, one gently and the other somewhat harder, almost the only difference between the two resulting sounds will be that one is soft and only just audible, whereas the other is loud and can be heard at a distance. The second possible difference between two musical sounds is that one may be higher in pitch than another. This is the main difference between two notes such as middle C and the C above on a piano. It is possible to strike them so that they sound equally loud, but differ as sounds because one is higher up the scale than the other. Lastly, the third difference between musical sounds is that one may differ in quality from another. This is the difference between two notes, which may be equal in pitch and loudness, but have been produced by different instruments, such as a piano and a violin.

These three factors—loudness, pitch, and quality—provide the most convenient method of differentiating between all sounds. They can be regarded as three ways in which sounds can differ. Whenever you hear two sounds it is possible to describe the differences between them by comparing them in these three ways. For example, a tuning fork and an organ will produce sounds which we hear as differing in at least two of these ways. The sounds they produce may have the same pitch, but one sound is almost bound to be louder than the other, and each sound certainly has its own quality. On the other hand, when you hear the words *bed* and *bad* it is possible that they are being said on the same pitch and are equally loud; in this case they differ in only one respect, that of quality. One of the main purposes of this book is to provide a way of talking about sounds so that it is possible to give a physical description of the variations in air pressure corresponding to these differences. For the remainder of this chapter we shall examine the two simpler differences—those of loudness and pitch—and see if we can discover the different conditions of the air corresponding to each of them.

It is quite easy to see how it is that sounds differ in loudness. If you strike a tuning fork hard the prongs begin by making large vibrations which, as the sound dies away, gradually become smaller and smaller. Similarly a loud noise is produced by plucking a string hard or striking the notes on a piano forcibly. So it is reasonable to assume that a large movement of the source of sound produces a loud sound, and that a small movement results in a soft sound. If we consider this from the point of view of the vibrations of the air we see that a large movement of the source produces a large movement of the air particles. Or considering a sound as consisting of fluctuations in air pressure, a large movement of the source causes great fluctuations of air pressure. From the listener's point of view, these large fluctuations of air pressure cause a correspondingly large movement of the eardrum, and are interpreted as loud sounds.

Our method of diagramming sounds is to show how the air pressure increases and decreases. We can now see how to diagram a difference of loudness between two sounds. Figure 2.1 is a diagram of two sounds, one being a loud sound where the variations in air pressure are large, and the other a soft sound, where they are much smaller. Figure 2.2 is a diagram (somewhat exaggerated) of the variations in pressure accompanying a tuning fork which has been struck fairly hard and then allowed to come to rest. Immediately after the fork has been struck the resulting variations in air pressure become gradually less and less.

The extent of the maximum variation in air pressure from normal during a sound is called the *amplitude** of that sound.

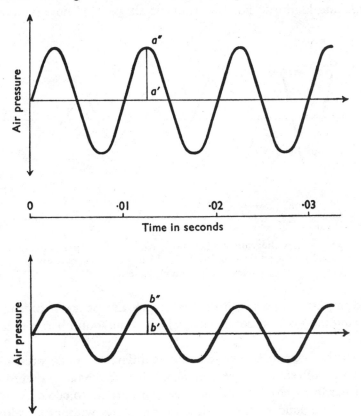

FIG. 2.1. Two sounds, one with twice the amplitude of the other.

In figure 2.1 the lines *a'*—*a"* and *b'*—*b"* represent the amplitudes of the two sounds. As you can see, in this case, one is about twice the other. Because the one amplitude is larger than the

* The reader is reminded that there is a glossary at the end of the book in which explanations are given of technical terms such as this.

other, the one sound is louder than the other. But owing to the nature of sound and the structure of our ears, we do not consider the one sound to be twice as loud as the other. Chapter 6 will give a more precise account of the relation between amplitude and loudness. For the moment all we need note is that if

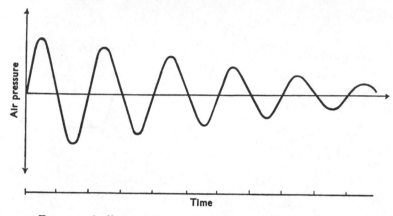

FIG. 2.2. A diagram (somewhat exaggerated) of part of the sound produced by a tuning fork which has been struck and is gradually coming to rest.

the amplitude of a sound decreases (i.e. the peaks of pressure. during the sound become weaker), then the sound becomes less loud.

The human ear is very sensitive to differences in air pressure. For the softest sound we can hear, the air pressure alongside our eardrum has to vary by only one part in 10,000,000,000; but for the loudest sounds that we can stand without a feeling of pain in our ears the pressure may be varying by more than a million times that amount.

The differences in the condition of the air corresponding to loud and soft sounds are much as we might expect. We know that we have to put more energy into making a loud noise than into making a soft one. It is hardly surprising that in a loud noise there is a bigger disturbance being transmitted through

the air, and consequently a greater movement of our eardrums.
There is, however, one point to be very careful about: in order
to build up a larger variation in air pressure, the particles
move farther and more rapidly. But this does not mean that
the peaks of pressure must occur more frequently. As you can
see in figure 2.1, although one sound has twice the amplitude
of the other, the peaks of pressure in both of them are still
occurring at the same rate of one every one hundredth of a
second. One of the two tuning forks may be making larger
vibrations than the other, but they are both making the same
number of complete vibrations a second.

In order to make this point quite clear it is worth while
conducting a simple experiment. If you make two pendulums,
each consisting of about a yard of string with a weight tied on
one end, they will both take about two seconds to make a
complete swing. Now if you start one pendulum by pulling it
only slightly to one side, and the other by pulling it much
farther to one side, the one will be making vibrations of small
amplitude, and the other vibrations of large amplitude. But
they will nevertheless both be making about the same number
of swings in a minute. If one is making fewer vibrations per
minute than the other (because the string is longer), it will
always vibrate that way no matter how hard you push it. The
time taken for a complete swing (of a pendulum or of a tuning
fork) does not depend on the amplitude or size of each swing.

If we do vary the rate at which a tuning fork is vibrating,
then we vary the rate at which peaks of pressure occur (as
opposed to the strength of each peak, which is the amplitude).
When we do this, we find that we are causing differences
between sounds in one of the other ways, namely, that of pitch.
The difference between a tuning fork of high pitch and one of
low pitch is that the higher pitched one is making a greater
number of vibrations per second. Consequently a diagram of a
high note as compared with a low note is as shown in figure 2.3.
Both sounds have peaks of pressure of the same amplitude;

but, as you can see from the time scale, in the one they are occurring every 1/100 of a second, whereas in the other they occur more frequently, viz. every 1/300 of a second.

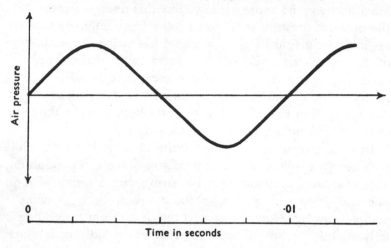

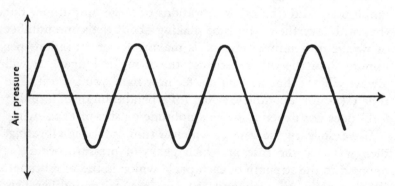

FIG. 2.3. Two sounds with equal amplitudes, but one with a frequency of 100 cps. and the other with a frequency of 300 cps.

The variations in air pressure in any sound that has a definite pitch must form a pattern which is repeated at regular intervals of time. In the case of the tuning forks which we have been discussing, the pattern consists of an increase to a peak of pressure, followed by a decrease to a minimum before again rising to normal. A complete variation in air pressure of this sort is called a *cycle*. Thus a cycle is the variation in pressure from the moment when the pressure changes in a certain manner, to the next moment when it changes in precisely the same way and starts to go through the same pattern of changes again. A cycle occurs every 1/100 of a second for the first sound in figure 2.3, and every 1/300 of a second for the other sound. Therefore there must be, in the first case 100 cycles per second, and in the second case 300 cycles per second. This rate at which cycles occur is known as the *frequency*. The two sounds in question have frequencies of 100 cycles per second (usually abbreviated to cps.) and 300 cps. For most practical purposes we can say that the pitch depends on the frequency or rate of repetition of the variations in air pressure. The second sound in figure 2.3 has a higher pitch than the first because it has a higher frequency—i.e. during the second sound there are a greater number of complete variations in air pressure (complete cycles) in one second than there are during the first sound.

In order to understand the difference between frequency and amplitude it is seriously suggested that the reader should perform the experiment with the two pendulums, as described on page 17. He will then discover that a given pendulum will vibrate with varying amplitude, but with a constant frequency. It will always take the same length of time to make one swing backwards and forwards (i.e. one cycle), irrespective of the size of the swing. The corresponding acoustic fact is that a given tuning fork may produce relatively large or small peaks of pressure, but each complete variation in air pressure will have the same duration. Thus the cycle of variations in air pressure will always be repeated the same number of times each second; or, in other words, the frequency of the sound will always be the same. Putting this in our everyday language, we can say that the sounds produced by a given tuning fork will all have the same pitch, although they may vary in loudness. Only by altering the length of the pendulum or the size of tuning fork can we alter the duration of each cycle, and so vary the frequency.

Whenever a definite pitch can be assigned to a sound the air is being made to vibrate in a regular manner. For example, when a tuning fork of a standard pitch A is struck, compressions and rarefactions occur in the surrounding air at a rate of 440 a second; each wave of compression follows exactly 1/440 seconds after the preceding one. Consequently, if our eardrums are affected by such a sound, they move backwards and forwards 440 times in a second.

Sounds with a low pitch have a low frequency; accordingly many of the sources of sound that produce low notes are large and heavy things which vibrate slowly. Just as a long pendulum vibrates more slowly than a short one, so a large bell has a lower frequency of vibration—consequently produces a lower note—than a small bell. Similarly the long heavy strings of a piano are at the bass, while the higher frequency notes at the treble end are produced by smaller strings. Sometimes when listening to the very low notes of an organ, one gets the impression that one can feel, and can almost count, the separate peaks of air pressure. This kind of sensation never occurs when listening to a high note.

When a note is exactly twice the frequency of another note it is said to be an octave higher. Thus standard pitch A on a piano is 440 cps.; the A above it (often written a′) is 880 cps.; and A above that (a″) is 1,760 cps. Remember that these figures correspond to the frequency of occurrence of the cycles of air pressure. These will occur at a similar rate to the frequency of vibration of the source of the sound, and the frequency of vibration of our eardrums. The lowest frequency which our ears can detect as a sound is about 16–20 cps. The highest frequency we can hear is about 20,000 cps.; above that frequency we cannot detect sounds, probably because our eardrums and the chain of connecting bones cannot vibrate fast enough. The student of speech, however, is primarily concerned with frequencies far below this. The fastest vibration a telephone can transmit is about 3,500 cps. Most of the frequencies of interest in the analysis of speech are below 8,000 cps.

The frequency of a note can be varied in different ways. As we have noted, other things being equal, a tuning fork with long prongs vibrates more slowly (i.e. produces a note of lower frequency) than a fork with short prongs. Similarly a long stretched string as on a double bass vibrates more slowly than the shorter string on a violin, which is consequently higher in pitch. Another way of altering the frequency of a string is to increase the tension. Thus a violinist tuning his instrument tightens or loosens the strings so as to raise or lower the frequency.

Finally, variation in the mass of a vibrating body will affect the frequency. A heavy string of a given length and under a certain tension will vibrate more slowly than an equally taut light string of the same length.

We usually use the word *pitch* when we are referring to that aspect of a sound whereby we can, using only our ears, place it on a scale going from low to high. When we are discussing actual rates of vibration or rates of fluctuations in air pressure, we speak of the *frequency* of the sound. Similarly *loudness* is the term we use when we are describing one of the ways in which we can hear sounds to differ. It corresponds (more or less) to the instrumentally measurable factor which we call the *intensity* of the sound. The intensity is derivable from the *amplitude* or amount of increase in pressure during a sound. In a subsequent chapter we shall have to expand and qualify these remarks. But for the moment we can take it that when only the frequency of a sound is altered, then only the pitch is varied. Similarly when the amplitude of a sound is increased while the frequency remains unaltered, then we hear an increase in loudness.

3

Quality

In the last chapter we saw how variation in pitch and loudness occurred. Now we must consider differences in quality. We must try to explain, for instance, the differences between middle C played on a piano and on a violin; or how it is possible to make different vowel sounds on the same pitch.

So far we have considered in detail only one type of musical note—that produced by a tuning fork. Now the back and forth movements of the prongs of a tuning fork are fairly steady and regular. As we saw in Chapter 1, a point attached to the prong of a sounding tuning fork will draw a smooth curve as it is moved over a sheet of paper. The technical name for a mathematically specified wave very similar to this is a *sine wave*.

Not all sounds have such simple wave forms as those produced by tuning forks. This is because most sources of sound vibrate in a far more complex way. Figure 3.1 shows the wave shape that occurs when a note (in this case the C below middle C) is played on a piano. Remember that this diagram means that if we could measure the air pressure we would find that it went up and down in the way shown. If you were listening to this note the air pressure alongside your eardrum would be at one moment high, then it would decrease to nearly normal, then it would waver up and down, tending to fall all the time, before again sharply rising to its maximum. A microphone used in conjunction with other electric equipment can record these changes in air pressure. This diagram is based on a photograph of air-pressure measurements made with the aid of a microphone placed a short distance away from a piano.

When there are such complex fluctuations of pressure the

particles of air must be moving in a complicated way. When they were agitated by the vibrations of a tuning fork they merely moved backwards and forwards in the simple way we have already described. Their motion corresponded to that of the bob of a pendulum; from their maximum position of displacement they started slowly, gradually increasing their speed until they reached their normal position, and from there on slowing down until they reached their maximum displace-

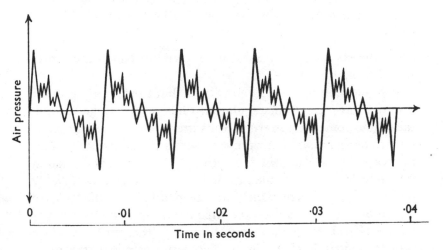

FIG. 3.1. The wave form of the C below middle C on a piano.

ment in the other direction. As we have seen this kind of movement corresponds to fluctuations in air pressure which can be represented by means of the smooth curves known as sine waves.

But the variations in air pressure which occur when a note on a piano is played are far more complex. In other words the movements of the air particles conveying this sound are very complex. And this, in turn, is due to the complex way in which a piano string vibrates. Unlike the prongs of a tuning fork which simply move backwards and forwards, a stretched string can be made to vibrate in several ways at once. Figure 3.2 is a diagram which shows how different parts of a string can be vibrating in different ways at the same time. The strings of a piano vibrate in a complex way such as this, and consequently

FIG. 3.2. Solid line: one position of a vibrating string. Dashed line: another position, giving an impression of vibration of parts of the string. Taken as a whole the string may be said to vibrate in many ways at the same time.

cause the complex variations in air pressure which are represented in figure 3.1.

If you look at figure 3.1 you will see that the variations in air pressure have a certain regularity. Once every 1/130 second, the whole complex pattern repeats itself. As we said earlier, a pattern of variations in air pressure which is repeated at regular intervals of time is known as a cycle; and the pitch of the sound is largely dependent on the rate at which the cycles recur. In the particular wave form which we are considering the rate of repetition of the cycles—the frequency—is 130 cycles per second. If this frequency were increased, the pitch would be raised; conversely if the frequency were decreased, the pitch would become lower. Nearly all the diagrams of sound waves in this book include a time scale. Accordingly it is usually possible to calculate the fundamental frequency of repetition of the sound waves. The reader should check that when the text refers to e.g. a 100 cps. wave, the diagram shows a wave form which repeats itself every 0.01 second as indicated by the time scale.

The difference between the qualities of the sounds of a tuning fork and of a piano is due to the difference in the complexity of the wave form. Whenever sounds differ in quality we find that they have different wave shapes. Figure 3.3 shows the wave shapes produced when the author pronounced the

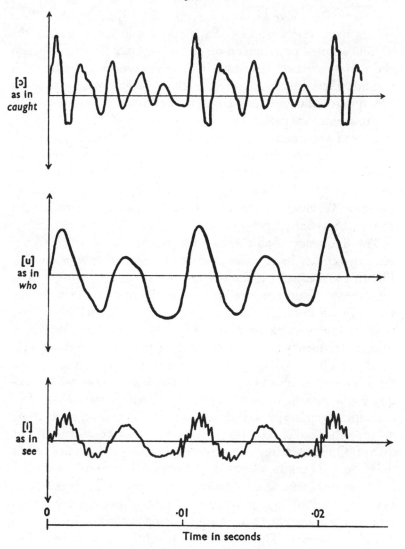

[ɔ]
as in
caught

[u]
as in
who

[i]
as in
see

0   ·01   ·02

Time in seconds

FIG. 3.3. The wave form produced when the author pronounced the vowels [ɔ] as in *caught*, [u] as in *who* and [i] as in
see with a constant pitch (fundamental frequency 100 cps.).
In this, and all the following figures unless otherwise noted, the
vertical scale represents variations in air pressure.

vowels* [i] as in *see* [ɔ] as in *caught,* and [u] as in *who.* These
waves have very complex shapes; but you can see that the
vowels were all pronounced on the same pitch; in each of them
the complex pattern repeats itself every one hundredth of a
second. The differences between these vowel sounds are all in
the quality dimension. They are heard as different vowels
because each has a characteristic wave shape.

One of the main objects of this book is to build up a way
of describing sound waves. We have seen how to specify the
pitch in terms of the frequency, or number of vibrations per
second, and the loudness in terms of the amplitude, or peaks of
pressure. We now have to try to describe quality in terms of the
complex wave shapes.

The frequency of all these vowels is 100 cps., since the main
pattern repeats itself once every one hundredth of a second.
But in each vowel we can see one or two other more or less
regular waves superimposed on top of the main pattern. In the
vowel [ɔ] as in *caught* this added wave repeats itself about five
times for every single repetition of the main pattern. We know
that the frequency of repetition of the complex wave is 100 cps.
So the smaller wave in [ɔ] has a frequency of around 500 cps.
Similarly in the vowel [u] as in *who* there is a wave whose frequency is nearly twice that of the fundamental frequency;
consequently it is approximately 200 cps. The vowel [i] as in *see*
on the other hand, has two waves which can be separated out
by eye. One has a frequency of 200 cps. since it occurs about
twice during each repetition of the complex pattern. The other
is a wave representing a far more rapid variation in air pressure.
It looks as if it were superimposed on top of the 200 cps. wave,
and occurs about thirty-five times during each repetition of the
complex pattern. The frequency of this wave is therefore
about 3,500 cps.

We can now see how differences in quality may be described.

* The phonetic symbols used in this book are those of the International Phonetic
Association's alphabet.

The vowels [i] *see*, [ɔ] *caught*, and [u] *who*, when they are all said on the same pitch (100 cps.) are characterized by the presence of additional frequencies; the approximate values of the principal extra frequencies are 500 cps. for [ɔ], 200 cps. for [u], and 200 cps. and 3,500 cps. for [i]. This is, of course, a gross over-simplification of the situation. As we shall see later, complex sounds like vowels actually have to be described as consisting of far more than two or three frequencies. But this method of analysis by visual inspection provides a useful basis for a preliminary description.

If we now try to synthesize these vowels by sounding a number of pure tones simultaneously, we can see the failings in this form of analysis. Let us suppose we try to synthesize the vowel [ɔ] *caught* by sounding a fairly loud tuning fork of 100 cps. (because this was the basic frequency of repetition of the complex wave shape) plus an additional tuning fork with a frequency of 500 cps. (because this was the main superimposed frequency that was characteristic of this vowel). Figure 3.4 is a diagram of the variations in air pressure which result when these two forks are sounded separately. When they are sounded together the air pressure is affected by both of them. Figure 3.5 is a diagram of this situation. The dotted lines represent the pressure variations that would be produced by the individual forks, and the solid line represents the composite wave form that results. As you can see, when both forks are working to-gether to increase the pressure (as at the times marked *a*) the resultant pressure is above that produced by either alone; similarly when both forks are working together to decrease the pressure the resulting pressure is less than that which would result from the action of either fork alone; but when the two forks are working against each other, one trying to increase the pressure while the other is trying to decrease it (as at the times marked *b*), the resultant pressure is somewhere between the two.

The wave shape in figure 3.5, however, is not very similar

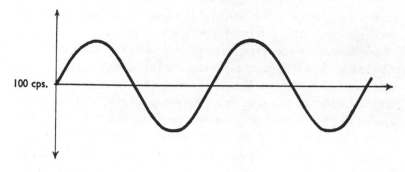

100 cps.

500 cps.

FIG. 3.4. The variations in air pressure which result when two tuning forks, one with a frequency of 100 cps. and the other with a frequency of 500 cps., are sounded separately.

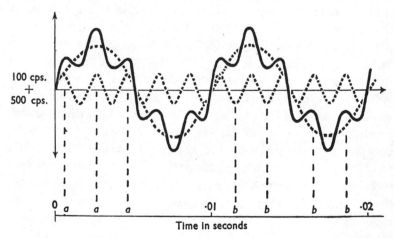

100 cps.
+
500 cps.

0   a   a   a   ·01   b   b   b   b   ·02

Time in seconds

FIG. 3.5. The complex wave which results when the two waves shown in fig. 3.4 are superimposed.

to the wave shape of the vowel [ɔ] in figure 3.3. But this is hardly surprising, since two tuning forks sounded together do not sound like a vowel. These two wave shapes, which may represent variations in air pressure alongside our ears (and consequently are directly related to the movements of our eardrums), are not the wave shapes of identical sounds. The wave shape of any vowel is far more complex than that of two tuning forks.

In our study of the acoustics of speech sounds we shall have to consider wave shapes that are even more complex than those of vowels. Figure 3.6 is a diagram of the sound wave which

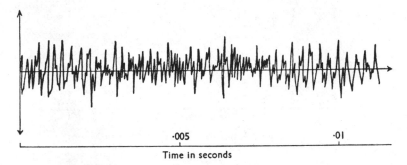

·005   ·01

Time in seconds

FIG. 3.6. The sound wave which occurred during the pronunciation of the last part of the word *hiss*.

occurs during the last part of the word *hiss*. We can, as usual, take it as a representation of the changes in air pressure which occur alongside our eardrums. These changes will, of course, cause movements of the eardrum which will be perceived by the brain as sounds. But, unlike all the other sounds we have considered so far, the movements of the eadrum will be irregular, since the air pressure goes up and down in an irregular manner.

It is often convenient to consider sounds in which the variations in air pressure do not follow a regular pattern as being in a different class from those in which there is a cycle of variations

in air pressure which is exactly repeated at regular intervals of
time. Figure 3.7 is a diagram of another sound with a non-
repetitive wave form. Note especially that although the variations in air pressure that occur during the period from time *a*
to time *b* are similar to those which occur during the period

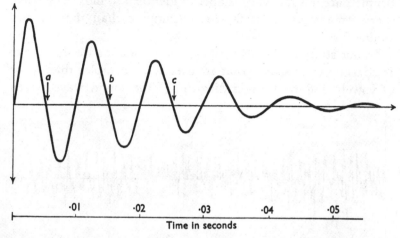

Time in seconds

FIG. 3.7. A non-repetitive wave form.

from time *b* to time *c*, their amplitude is distinctly greater,
and therefore they are not identical. In this sound there is no
pattern of variations in air pressure which is *exactly* repeated at
regular intervals of time.

Of course, if we are being precise in our discussion of sounds,
we must admit that every sound we have discussed so far (and,
indeed, every sound we are ever likely to discuss) has in fact a
non-repetitive wave form. In no real sound is there a pattern
of variations in air pressure which is repeated *exactly* at regular
intervals of time for ever and ever. As we have seen, even the
vibrations of a tuning fork die away eventually; consequently
each wave has a little less amplitude, and is not precisely the
same as the wave that preceded it. Moreover, the fork is set in
motion by a blow; until a steady state of vibration has been

reached, the waves are far from exactly repetitive. However, the errors resulting from disregarding these factors are very small. We shall, as a matter of convenience, consider some sounds to have cycles of variations in air pressure which are repeated exactly at regular intervals of time, whereas other sounds we shall consider to have non-repetitive wave forms. (The distinction between these two classes of sounds is considered further on page 48.)

Both classes of sounds are of great interest to the student of speech. As we know, spoken words consist of sounds which are continually changing in quality. Sometimes, as at the beginning and end of the word *peak*, the wave form is altering very rapidly. The variations in air pressure which affect our ears are very sudden and irregular; consequently we shall consider the word *peak* to begin and end with a non-repetitive wave form. In comparison with such sounds, the middle part of the word *peak* lasts for an appreciable length of time without much alteration in quality; we shall therefore consider this part of the word to consist of regular variations in air pressure.

One of the characteristics of sounds with non-repetitive wave forms is that they cannot be said to have any precise pitch. As we saw earlier, the pitch of a sound is largely dependent on the frequency with which the cycle of variations in air pressure is repeated. Sounds in which no part of the wave form is exactly and constantly repeated do not have any definite pitch. When we listen to the irregular variations in air pressure caused by the striking of a match or the rustling of leaves, we find that we can say very little about the pitch of these sounds. Nor do the non-repetitive wave forms at the beginning and end of the word *peak* produce any precise sensations of pitch. If this word can be said to have been spoken on a definite pitch, it is due to the more regular variations in air pressure which occur in the middle part of the word.

The main difference between this book and other books on acoustics is that we are more concerned with non-repetitive

wave forms. We shall have to deal with all sorts of sounds varying from those which have no pattern at all in their wave form,
to those where the wave form is almost, but not quite, exactly
repetitive. There is actually a special name for the sound with
the most complex wave form. It is called *white noise*. The name
is due to the analogy of white light, which is light that is made
up of all the colours of the rainbow. White noise is a complex
sound composed of equal amounts of all audible tones. The
nearest approach to it with which we are all familiar is the
background hiss which occurs on a radio.

Several sounds occur in speech which are almost as complex
as white noise. We have already mentioned the sound that
occurs at the end of the word *hiss*. Other sounds of this sort
occur at the beginning and end of the word *fish*.

A somewhat less complex wave form, which is also of great
interest to us in our study of speech, is shown in figure 3.8.

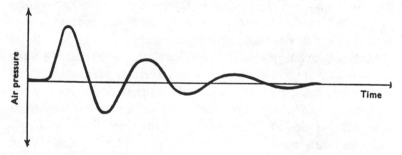

FIG. 3.8. The sound wave produced when a bottle is given a tap.

This is the sort of sound that occurs when you tap a bottle.
The diagram indicates that the air pressure varies in a fairly
regular way but the amplitude of each peak of pressure is
considerably less than the amplitude of the preceding peak of
pressure.

Finally, we must consider here the sound corresponding to
a very sharp tap on some object which has little or no tendency
to vibrate. If the tap were sharp enough, it might cause the air

pressure to rise rapidly, and then to fall away again equally
rapidly as shown in figure 3.9. The nearest approach to this
sort of sound is the click that occurs when we switch a loud-
speaker on or off.

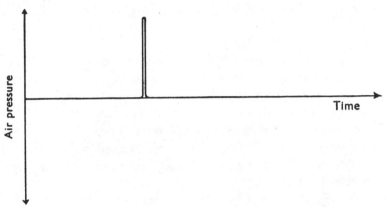

FIG. 3.9. The sound wave of a very sharp tap or click.

In other books on acoustics the word transient is sometimes
used to describe a specific group of the sounds which we have
been discussing above. However, in this book this term will be
avoided, as it has been found to cause confusion. As we shall
see in the next chapter, the division of all sounds into two
classes, depending on whether they can be considered to have
a non-repetitive wave form or not, is made for convenience in
analysis. It would certainly be useful if there were a general
term which could be used to describe all sounds with non-
repetitive wave forms, including a hissing noise which goes on
for some considerable time, a dull thud which occurs when a
falling object hits the ground, and a click which is the result of
a single sharp variation in air pressure. As, however, there is no
accepted generic term for all these sounds, we shall have to
continue to describe them as *sounds which can be considered to have
non-repetitive wave forms*—a somewhat cumbersome phrase, but
one that cannot be avoided.

4

Wave Analysis

We saw in the last chapter that two pure tones can combine to produce a complex wave shape. What is not so easy to see is that any wave form whatsoever can be synthesized from a sufficient number of pure tones. The wave forms of the vowels in figure 3.3 and the non-repetitive wave forms which we discussed at the end of the last chapter can all be synthesized provided we take enough pure tones and combine them in an appropriate manner.

The method of analysis in which a complex wave is regarded as a suitable combination of a number of pure tones is known as Fourier analysis. The theorem underlying it was discovered by the French mathematician Fourier in 1822. It is such a basic concept in acoustics that it is worth while considering one or two further examples.

We may start by combining a 100 cps. wave with a small 200 cps. wave and a somewhat larger 300 cps. wave. The result is shown in figure 4.1. The complex wave is simply the result of adding the increases in air pressure (i.e. those points on the curve above the line representing normal pressure) and subtracting the decreases in air pressure (those points below the line). At time x, for instance, two of the pure tones were causing increases in pressure of amounts represented by the lines a and b; whereas the third was causing a decrease in pressure of amount represented by the line c. The resultant air pressure has an amplitude represented by the line d whose length is equivalent to $a+b-c$. Similarly at time y the resultant air pressure is $-g$ (minus because it is below the line; i.e. the point represents a moment of rarefaction or decrease in pressure).

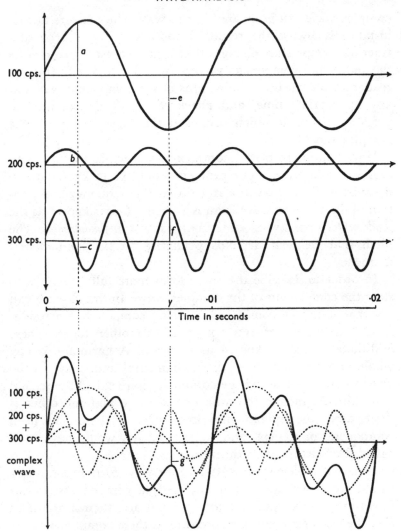

FIG. 4.1. A combination of 100 cps., 200 cps. and 300 cps. waves forming a complex wave.

In this case $-g = -e + f$. The 200 cps. component has no effect at this moment, as its amplitude is zero. Any point in the complex wave can be treated in this way. The pressure at that instance is always the result of combining (adding or subtracting) the pressure changes that would have been caused by the individual component waves. In order to verify this the reader should measure the heights of the component waves at any appropriate time, and check that they do combine to produce the point which occurs at the same instant on the complex wave.

If we had intercepted a complex wave such as we have synthesized in figure 4.1, our problem would be to know how to describe it. First of all we can see that the frequency of repetition of the complex wave form is 100 cps. This is known as the *fundamental frequency*, or sometimes just as the *fundamental*. The pitch that we hear depends primarily on the fundamental frequency.

In order to describe the wave form more fully we have to state the components of the complex wave. In this case we can say that it can be considered as being composed of a fundamental frequency of 100 cps. plus two other tones. These additional tones are known as *harmonics*. A harmonic is any whole number multiple of the fundamental frequency. In the wave we are considering the components are called the second and third harmonics, because one is twice and the other is three times the fundamental frequency. If there had been components of 400 cps. and 1,000 cps., they would have been called the fourth and tenth harmonics.*

A more complete specification of the wave form in figure 4.1 would state not only the frequencies of the components (in this case 100 cps., 200 cps., and 300 cps.) but also their amplitudes (i.e. the size of the peaks of pressure in these components). As we have drawn it, the fundamental frequency is the largest of

---

* In some of the older textbooks on acoustics the component with a frequency twice that of the fundamental is called the *first* harmonic and the component with a frequency three times that of the fundamental is called the *second* harmonic, etc. We reject this old habit because its arithmetic is confusing, like the French "8-days" for "a week" and "15 days" for "a fortnight".

the three, the second harmonic is considerably smaller, and the
third is about three-fifths the size of the fundamental. If we
represented the relative amplitudes of the components by the
relative lengths of lines, we could draw a diagram as shown in
figure 4.2. This kind of diagram is of considerable importance

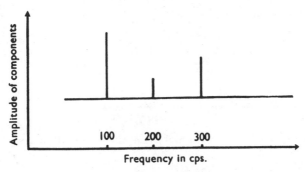

FIG. 4.2. The spectrum of the complex wave illustrated
in fig. 4.1.

in acoustics. It is called the *spectrum* of a sound. It is a statement
of the components of a sound and thus provides a simpler
description than is given by a diagram of the complex wave
shape.

It is possible to draw a diagram of the spectrum of any sound.
For instance, when we were trying to synthesize the vowel [ɔ]
caught by sounding two tuning forks (figure 3.5) we could have
drawn a diagram of the situation in the form shown in figure
4.3. The complex wave we produced had two components,
one being a 100 cps. wave (the fundamental) and the other
being a 500 cps. wave (the fifth harmonic of the fundamental).
The relative amplitudes of the components were 3 to 1, i.e. the
fundamental was much more powerful than the harmonic.
All this information is conveyed by the diagram in figure 4.3.
Similarly we could draw a diagram of the components of the
complex wave produced by a piano. The C below middle C,
whose wave form was illustrated in figure 3.1, can be described

in terms of the spectrum shown in figure 4.4. This shows that
the complex wave may be considered as being composed of a
fundamental and a large number of harmonics. Apart from the

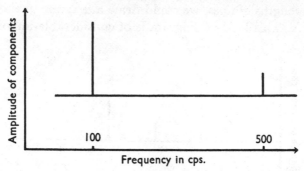

FIG. 4.3. The spectrum of the complex wave illustrated
in fig. 3.5.

fifteenth and sixteenth harmonics, which are missing or too
faint to show up, all the harmonics up to the eighteenth play a
part in building up the complex wave. Note that in these diagrams only the frequency scale is calibrated. No absolute values

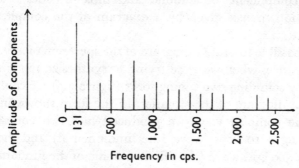

FIG. 4.4. The spectrum of the wave form illustrated in
fig. 3.1, the C below middle C on a piano.

for the amplitudes are marked, because the shape of the complex wave is determined by the relative strength of the components. When the amplitude of a complex wave is increased

(i.e. when the sound becomes louder) the amplitudes of all the components are increased in the same proportion.

A diagram of the spectrum of a sound does leave out some of the information that is present in the complex wave. In some senses it is a simplification since it does not tell us everything about the way in which the components are combined. In figure 4.1 the components were drawn so that at the point at which the diagram starts the component waves were all about to cause an increase in pressure. But now suppose that these pure tones (which may represent sounds accompanying tuning forks) were not combined in this way. If we are thinking in terms of a wave which we have synthesized, it is quite conceivable that one tuning fork should have been started before the others. Consequently, at the time when they were brought close together (which may be thought of as time zero on the diagram), the situation might be as in figure 4.5. Here, at the start of the diagram, the tuning fork with the lowest frequency is about to cause an increase in pressure, the second tuning fork is producing a wave which is about to decline from a peak of maximum pressure, and the third tuning fork is about to cause a decrease in pressure. If we now combine the pressure variations, as we did on the previous occasions, the resulting complex wave is as shown. At any moment the pressure of the complex wave is the result of adding or subtracting the pressure of the components. For example, at the times marked a and b the variation from normal air pressure is zero, because at these points the pressure changes caused by the components cancel out.

This complex wave form repeats itself one hundred times a second. In this respect it is the same as the wave in figure 4.1; but in other ways these waves look very different. Yet each of them has components with the same frequencies and amplitudes. The difference is due solely to the way in which these components are combined. This difference in the timing of the components is known as a difference of *phase*.

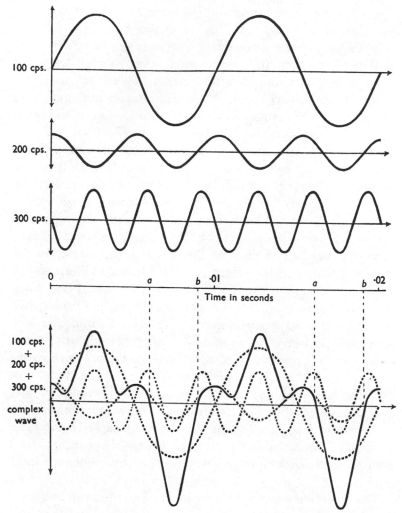

FIG. 4.5. A combination of 100 cps., 200 cps. and 300 cps. waves, differing from the combination in fig. 4.1 in respect of their relative timing, and consequently forming a different complex wave.

Because the waves in figures 4.1 and 4.5 can be analysed into the same components, the diagrams of their spectra will be the same. The spectrum of a sound shows only which frequencies are present, and with what amplitudes; it does not usually specify the way in which the components are combined. Figure 4.2 is therefore the spectrum corresponding to both the wave in figure 4.1 and that in figure 4.5, since it designates a sound with a fundamental of 100 cps. combined with a second harmonic with 3/10 of the amplitude of the fundamental and a third harmonic with 3/5 the amplitude of the fundamental.

It is possible to produce, by electrical means, pure tones which may be combined so as to make either of the wave forms corresponding to the spectrum shown in figure 4.2. It is even possible to alter the way in which the pure tones are combined, so that the wave form of figure 4.1 changes slowly into that of figure 4.5, passing through a variety of other wave forms on the way. The astonishing thing is that our ears can hear no difference between all these wave forms. As long as the components stay the same, the sound will be the same. Apart from special cases involving very loud sounds (which are probably irrelevant as far as the acoustics of speech is concerned), the quality of a sound does not depend on the way in which the components are combined; it depends simply on the frequencies and the amplitudes of the component waves.

We can now see why it is that the wave form does not provide a satisfactory method of describing the quality of a sound. We may consider two sounds to be identical because they have the same components; but they may nevertheless have very different wave forms. Moreover it is possible for any sound (e.g. the vowel [i] as in see) to have one wave form on one occasion, and to have a different wave form on another occasion. We should hear both sounds as being the same vowel provided the components of these different waves were the same. Consequently it is often better to represent a sound by a diagram showing its spectrum, rather than by a diagram of its wave form. The spectrum of the vowel [i] as in see will always be the same as long as the components are the same.

In recent years it has become possible to produce an instrumental display of sound spectra. Since then the science of acoustics has been able to give far more help to students of speech. Previously the best method of making sounds visible was by means of a cathode ray oscillograph. This is an instrument which provides a picture of the wave form by producing a graph of the variations in air pressure on a screen somewhat similar to that of a television tube. It was used as a basis for many of the diagrams in this book. But, as we have seen, it is difficult to study sounds by reference to the complex wave shapes. The mathematical analysis of the curves is possible but it is a lengthy process. It is only now that we can find the spectra of sounds by means of an instrument known as a sound spectrograph* that we can make any real progress in the acoustic description of speech sounds.

So far all our analyses have been of sounds that have a definite frequency. But it is also possible to specify the spectra of

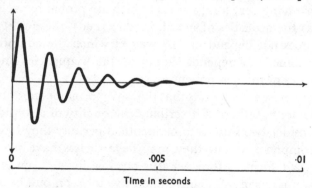

Time in seconds

Fig. 4.6. A non-repetitive wave form in which peaks of pressure occur at the rate of 1,000 a second for as long as the sound lasts.

sounds with non-repetitive wave forms, such as that shown in figure 4.6. This wave can be analysed into a number of pure

* The use of this instrument is discussed at length in the author's forthcoming introduction to experimental phonetics: *Speech in the Laboratory*.

tones (which are, of course, regular waves) in much the same way as the repetitive wave forms which we have been considering in this chapter up till now.

If we examine the wave form in figure 4.6 we can see that, while the sound lasts, peaks of pressure occur every one thousandth of a second. Consequently we may well expect to find that one component of this sound has a frequency of 1,000 cps. All we have to find in addition are some components which will cause the amplitude of the complex wave to become less and less.

It turns out that if we add to the 1,000 cps. wave one component with a slightly lower frequency and another with a slightly higher frequency, we achieve something like the result we desire. These two waves, along with the 1,000 cps. wave, are shown in the upper part of figure 4.7. One of them has a frequency of 900 cps. and the other a frequency of 1,100 cps.; both have amplitudes half as large as the 1,000 cps. wave. The result of combining these three waves for a limited time is shown in the lower part of figure 4.7.

As you can see in the figure, at time *a* both these waves are assisting the 1,000 cps. component to increase the pressure; consequently the first peak of pressure is fairly large. At time *b*, they are both assisting, but not so much, so that the second peak is somewhat smaller. At time *c* they almost cancel each other out, their combined effect being to cause only a slight increase in the peak of pressure due to the 1,000 cps. wave alone. At time *d* they are causing a small decrease in the maximum pressure. This effect is enhanced at time *e*, when they are causing a considerable lowering in the peak of pressure. These three waves therefore can be combined for a short period to produce a wave shape similar to the wave form we wished to analyse.

As the complex wave shown in figure 4.7 looks very like the complex wave in figure 4.6 it might seem that we could describe this wave form as having a spectrum similar to that shown in figure 4.8, i.e. as being composed of pure tones with

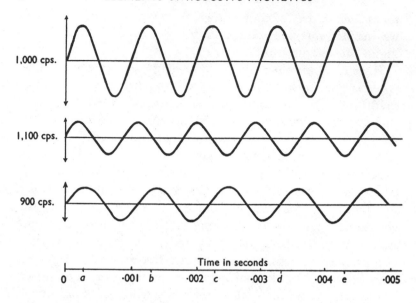

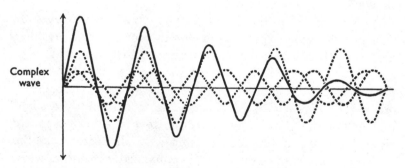

FIG. 4.7. A combination of 1,000 cps., 1,100 cps. and 900 cps. waves to form a complex wave.

frequencies of 900 cps., 1,000 cps., and 1,100 cps., the 900 cps. and 1,100 cps. tones each having amplitudes half that of the 1,000 cps. tone. However, this is not quite true as the complex wave in figure 4.7 is not exactly the same as the wave in figure 4.6. The latter sound started abruptly—presumably from silence—and then faded away—presumably into silence again. But the component waves which have to be added

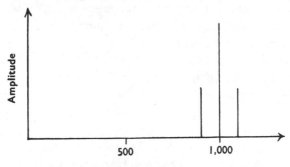

Frequency in cps.

FIG. 4.8. The spectrum of the complex wave in fig. 4.7.

together to make the complex wave in figure 4.7 are all pure tones—i.e. in each wave each cycle is the same as the following

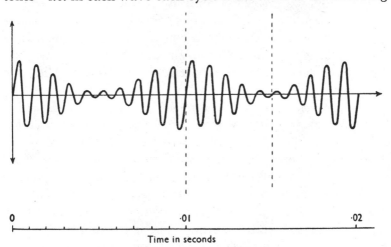

Time in seconds

FIG. 4.9. A complex wave (with a fundamental frequency of 100 cps.) composed of three waves with frequencies of 900, 1,000, and 1,100 cps. Fig. 4.7 showed only that part of this wave which is between the dashed lines.

one, which is the same as the next one, and so on, theoretically to infinity. But if the pure tones indicated in figure 4.7 were

combined for a longer period they would go on to produce a
wave form as shown in figure 4.9. The wave in figure 4.6 was
roughly the same as that part of the complex wave between the
dotted lines. Consequently we see that it would be only an
approximation to the truth to say that this wave form had the
spectrum shown in figure 4.8. An analysis of this wave form
into the three components shown in the spectrum makes no
pretence at taking into account the fact that the sound which
we set out to analyse had a sudden beginning and was followed
by silence. If we do make allowances for this fact, we find that
we have to analyse the wave form into a large (actually an
infinite) number of components. Naturally we cannot demon-
strate this by drawing out all these components. But by representing some of them we can indicate the shape of the spectrum
they would produce (figure 4.10). The more usual method of
diagramming these components is by means of a curve as
shown in figure 4.11. When we represent a sound by a curve
of this sort, we mean that it has a complex wave, with an infinite
number of components. The height of the curve at any point
represents the relative amplitude of the component with that
frequency.

It is outside the scope of this book to give a complete mathematical explanation showing why there are an infinite number
of components in the spectrum of a non-repetitive wave.
However, we may note in passing that the wave shown in
figure 4.9, which had components of 900, 1,000, and 1,100 cps.,
had a fundamental frequency of 100 cps., i.e. it repeated itself
every hundredth of a second. If the components had been 900,
950, 1,000, 1,050, and 1,100 the fundamental frequency would
have been 50 cps., since the wave form would have been
repeated every fiftieth of a second. If we add still more components with, say, frequencies of 900, 901, 902, 903, . . .
1,096, 1,097, 1,098, 1,099, 1,100 cps. we find that the complex
wave produced has a fundamental frequency of one cycle per
second. In order to produce a complex wave which repeats

itself even more slowly, we must add component frequencies
which are even closer together. If the wave form is to occur

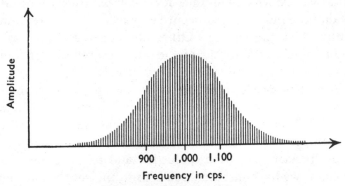

FIG. 4.10. A close approximation to the spectrum of the
sound wave shown in fig. 4.6.

only once in an infinite amount of time, i.e. it is never to repeat
itself, then the components must be infinitely close together.

It was pointed out at the end of the preceding chapter that
most of the sounds with which we are concerned are neither

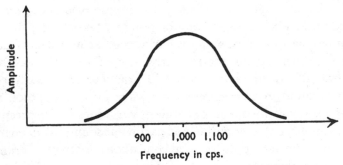

FIG. 4.11. The usual way of representing the spectrum
of the non-repetitive waveform shown in fig. 4.6.

non-repetitive wave forms preceded and followed by silence,
nor waves with a precise frequency of repetition. Instead they
consist of waves which are more or less like the waves before

and after them, the amount of their resemblance depending on the rate at which the quality is changing. Some speech sounds, such as vowels which continue for a comparatively long time, contain a number of consecutive waves which are almost identical with one another. Other parts of words, such as the abrupt beginning and end of the word *pat*, consist of sounds whose waves forms are altering very rapidly.

When we describe a sound wave by analysing it into its components we can either assume that it is one of an infinite number of identical waves (which is what we did in all our first analyses of complex waves), or we can assume that it is an isolated pressure variation, preceded and followed by silence (which, as we have just seen, leads us to the conclusion that it has an infinite number of components). When we are analysing a sound wave which is one of a number of similar consecutive waves, we usually use the first method. The sound is then said to have a *line spectrum*; on the other hand, when each wave is quite different from the adjacent waves, it is normally analysed by the second method. It is then said to have a *continuous spectrum*.

Earlier on (page 31) we stated that it is convenient to regard all sounds as belonging to one or other of two classes, the one class having wave forms that recur at regular intervals of time, and the other having non-repetitive wave forms. We can now see how this distinction is made in practice. We usually consider a sound to have a repetitive wave form as opposed to a wave form which consists of random variations in air pressure, if it is convenient to describe that particular sound by means of a line spectrum as opposed to a continuous spectrum. From a strictly mathematical point of view, all sounds should be described as having continuous spectra, since, in fact, all sounds have wave forms which are strictly speaking non-repetitive. But many sounds have wave forms which are so nearly exactly repetitive that we find it far more convenient to be able to describe them in terms of line spectra. When we analyse a nearly repetitive wave form in this way we obtain a simplified description in which the more important components are accurately specified, and only very minor components are neglected.

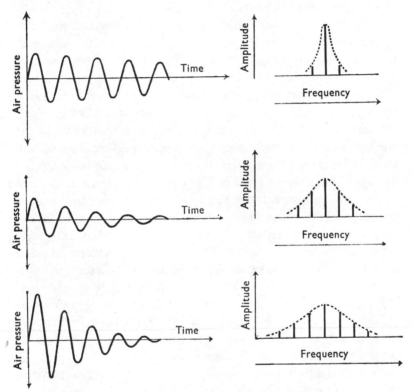

FIG. 4.12. Various waves and their spectra.

Figure 4.12 shows the analysis of various waves in both forms. Three different waves are shown on the left of the diagram and the spectra corresponding to each of them are shown on the right. The vertical lines in the spectra represent the components which could be considered as being present if the corresponding wave form was a single cycle of a complex wave which is repeated an infinite number of times; and the dotted curves in the diagrams of the spectra represent the results of the second form of analysis (i.e. regarding the corresponding wave form as a particular variation in air pressure which is preceded and followed by silence).

The first wave illustrated is nearly a pure tone. There is only a small decrease in amplitude between one peak and the next. Consequently, as we can see from the line spectrum, nearly all the energy of the complex wave is contained in the one component. The additional components which have to be combined with it have very small amplitudes. Similar information is conveyed in another way by the continuous spectrum in which we can see from the sharpness of the curve that most of the energy is concentrated in one frequency region. The second wave in figure 4.12 has a slightly more rapid rate of decay. Its line spectrum shows that it is composed of a greater number of tones with an appreciable amplitude; or, as we can see from the shape of the curve, the energy is not concentrated in such a narrow frequency region. The third wave dies away extremely rapidly. Many components of almost equal amplitudes are needed in order to synthesize a complex wave form of this sort; in other words, the energy is spread over a wide range of frequencies.

Now we can see why we can consider a tuning fork to be almost a pure tone. The rate of decay of a tuning fork is very slow, slower even than that of the first wave in figure 4.12. It is possible to strike a tuning fork of, say, the note A (440 cps.), so that it lasts for several seconds. Consequently it makes many thousand vibrations, each one being nearly the same as the preceding one. As a result, the wave form of a tuning fork can be analysed into one dominant pure tone with only very small additional components.

Many of the sounds of speech, on the other hand, die away within a few thousandths of a second. They are similar to the third wave in figure 4.12, and on analysis prove to be composed of a large number of pure tones with similar amplitudes.

The general rule to be remembered is that a sharp pointed

curve represents the spectrum of a sound with a slow rate of decay; since the energy in this sound is concentrated in one frequency region, it is nearly a pure tone. On the other hand, a non-repetitive wave form with a rapid rate of decay is represented by a much flatter curve, indicating that it contains energy spread over a wider range of frequencies.

Many speech sounds consist of regular repetitions of a cycle of variations in air pressure somewhat similar to the isolated pressure variations which we have been considering. Figure 4.13 shows on the left three waves (a, b, c) of this type, plus a fourth wave (d) which may be considered as being preceded and followed by silence. If this fourth wave represents the sound produced by a single tap on a bottle, then the other waves represent sounds produced by a series of taps recurring at regular intervals of time. As we shall see later, these "taps" correspond in speech sounds to the regular opening and closing of the vocal cords.

Earlier in this chapter we saw that when we analyse a repetitive wave so as to produce a line spectrum, we find that all the components have frequencies which are whole number multiples of the frequency of repetition of the complex wave form. So, in the case of wave (a) in figure 4.13, which rises to its peak amplitude once in every two hundredths of a second, the possible components are tones with frequencies of 200, 400, 600, . . . cps. The actual spectrum of this wave is shown on the right of the figure. The largest component has a frequency of 1,000 cps., which is just as might be expected, since we can see at a glance that in wave (a) small peaks of pressure occur every one thousandth of a second. Similar peaks of pressure recur every thousandth of a second in wave (d). But since this wave is considered as being preceded and followed by silence, it is analysed in terms of a continuous spectrum. In this spectrum, just as in the spectrum of wave (a), the component with the largest amplitude has a frequency of 1,000 cps. There are, moreover, other similarities between the spectra of these two waves: the relative amplitudes of all the components in the spectrum of wave (a) are exactly the same as the relative amplitudes of the corresponding components in wave (d).

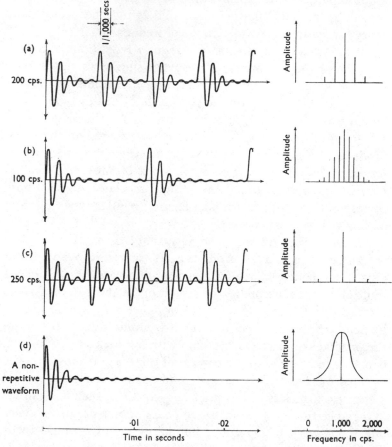

FIG. 4.13. Various waves and their spectra.

Thus the 800 cps. component has in each case half the amplitude of the 1,000 cps. component; and in both spectra, the 600 cps. components are very small.

When we consider waves (b) and (c) in figure 4.13 we find

that their spectra are also in some ways similar to the spectrum of wave (d). Wave (b) is a complex wave form recurring every hundredth of a second, and wave (c) is a complex wave form of a similar shape recurring 250 times a second. Consequently

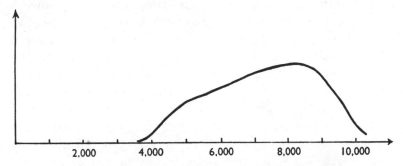

FIG. 4.14 (*a*). The spectrum of the sound which occurs at the end of the word *hiss*. In this and all following figures showing spectra the horizontal scale gives the frequency in cps.; the vertical dimension indicates the relative amplitude of the components.

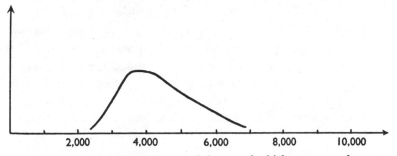

FIG. 4.14 (*b*). The spectrum of the sound which occurs at the end of the word *hush*.

the components in their spectra are multiples of 100 in the case of wave (b) and of 250 in the case of wave (c). Furthermore both these waves are similar to wave (a) in that they contain peaks of pressure which recur with diminishing amplitude every thousandth of a second. Consequently the components with the largest amplitudes in their spectra are at 1,000 cps.; and, as in the case of wave (a), all the other components that are present have the same relative amplitudes as in the spectrum of wave (d). We can draw an identical curve round the spectrum of each of the waves (a), (b), and (c); moreover, this curve has the same shape as the spectrum of wave (d), which is an isolated occurrence of a wave form similar to the repetitive wave forms contained in each of the other waves. This result will be important for us when we come to consider how the phonetic quality of a sound may stay the same despite variations in the pitch, which is, of course, dependent on the fundamental frequency.

We may conclude this chapter by considering the components which we would have to combine in order to build up the irregular wave forms that occur during the sounds at the ends of the words *hiss* and *hush*. If you listen to these two sounds you will hear that they both convey some sensation of pitch. They both have energy spread over a wide range of frequencies; but in neither case is it completely uniformly divided among the frequency components. Their spectra is shown in figure 4.14. In the sound at the end of the word *hiss* most of the component frequencies with any appreciable amplitude are above 6,600 cps. The sound at the end of *hush*, on the other hand, has a substantial amount of its energy divided among frequency components from about 3,000 cps. to about 4,500 cps. It is accordingly heard as the lower pitched of these two sounds.

5

Resonance

In the last few chapters the emphasis has been on the analysis of sound waves, rather than on their production. We must now consider some of the properties of sources of sounds.

All sources of sound are moving bodies. Some of them, like tuning forks and piano strings, have a natural tendency to vibrate. Once they have been struck they go on vibrating at a definite rate (or frequency) for a considerable time. Other sources of sound, like drums and table tops, have less tendency to vibrate. They make a noise when struck, but the vibrations die away fairly rapidly. Still other sources, such as telephone earpieces and loudspeakers, have virtually no natural frequency of vibration. Each move backwards and forwards has to be controlled by electric currents.

It is, of course, possible to make one vibrating body cause vibrations in another body. This happens when the base of a sounding fork is placed on the table. If you strike a tuning fork and then hold it in your hand while it is vibrating it makes only a soft sound. But as soon as you place the base of the fork on a table the sound becomes very much louder. The movements of the fork cannot cause large variations in air pressure because the prongs are fairly small, and the air, instead of being compressed, can easily move round the sides of the prongs. But when the base of the fork is placed on a table, the vibrations of the fork are transmitted to the table, which then vibrates so that a larger amount of air is affected. The energy which the fork is expending in its vibrations is changed into sound waves more efficiently by the large flat surface of the table.

This principle is employed in many musical instruments. A

vibrating string does not by itself cause a very large disturbance of the air. But when, as in a piano or a violin, the vibrations of the string are made to drive a sounding board or the body of the violin, a much louder sound results. However, we must note that neither the sounding board nor the body of the violin vibrate in the same way as the strings which are driving them. To some extent they each prefer their own natural mode of vibration.

We are all familiar with several objects other than musical instruments which have a tendency to vibrate at specific frequencies. Glasses, vases, and many other objects will give out a ringing note when struck. As is well known, these objects will also resound when the appropriate note is played on a piano. A glass can even be made to ring by singing a suitable note. It is often said that opera singers, who can sing an appropriate note very loudly and clearly, can make a glass vibrate so much that it shatters of its own accord.

A simpler example of this sort of phenomenon can be demonstrated with two identical tuning forks. If one fork is struck and then brought near another fork whose natural frequency of vibration is the same, the second fork will begin to vibrate. As soon as the second fork has been set in motion it will, of course, create a sound wave in the ordinary way. Even if the first fork is stopped by placing a finger upon it, the second fork, once it has been started, will go on vibrating till it comes to rest of its own accord. This phenomenon, whereby one body can be set in motion by the vibrations of another body, is known as *resonance*. The one body is said to *resonate* to the other body.

It is easy enough to understand how resonance occurs in the case of the two tuning forks. When the first fork has been struck it vibrates, causing variations in air pressure to spread outwards. These pressure variations are, as we have seen, the result of small movements of particles of air. When the pressure variations occur alongside the second fork the air particles there are vibrating in much the same way as the original fork.

These movements act as a series of small pushes on the second fork, which is consequently set in motion.

It is important to note that the second fork does not start sounding loudly as soon as the first fork has been struck. It takes a certain amount of time for the vibrations to build up to their maximum. The air particles move in such a way that each back-and-forth movement acts as a small blow whose effect is added to that of the previous blow. Because the two tuning forks have the same natural frequency of vibration, each of these small blows arrives at exactly the right moment, so that its effect is to increase the total amount of vibration.

This is perhaps made clearer by considering a parallel case which is more familiar. Suppose you wished to give a child a ride on a swing. You would begin by giving a small push so that the swing would move away from you. Then, when it had swung back towards you again and was at the top of its curve, you would give it another small push. This would increase the amplitude of its swing; and on the next occasion another small push would make the child swing even higher. With a number of small pushes you can build up a large movement of the swing. But it all depends on the timing of the small pushes or blows. If you tried to give the small added push to the swing when it was still coming towards you, you would slow it down, and not assist it. Only by waiting till the swing is about to move away from you can your push have the maximum effect. This is the situation with the two identical tuning forks. The first small blow imparts a very slight motion to the second tuning fork. But this fork, having been displaced from its position of rest, moves back again with its natural rate of vibration, and is just about to start a second swing when the second blow occurs. This blow, and all the subsequent ones, help to build up large vibrations. But obviously the second fork will vibrate only if the blows arrive at the appropriate moments. This will occur when the natural rates of vibration (or frequencies) of the tuning forks are the same.

We may now consider more complex cases of resonance, such as that of a glass ringing when the appropriate note is struck on a piano. Basically the same principle is in operation. The piano causes movements of the air particles, which set the glass vibrating. As we saw in the last chapter, the sound wave produced by a piano has a complex form. The spectrum (figure 4.4) shows that it was composed of a fundamental and a large number of harmonics, some of which were fairly powerful. If one of these components has the same frequency as the natural rate of vibration of the glass, it may be able to cause movements of the air which set the glass vibrating.

It may, at first, seem hard to understand that the sound waves produced by a piano are actually, in practice, equivalent to a number of simple waves. But this is in fact the case. A numerical example may make the matter clearer. Let us suppose we have a glass whose natural frequency of vibration is 1,046 cps. When a note with this frequency (c″) is played on a piano, the glass will be set vibrating. But it will also vibrate when the note c′ (523 cps.) is played. A piano note of this frequency contains a strong second harmonic, i.e. a component with a frequency of 2 × 523 cps. Because of this there will be appropriately timed movements of the air particles which can start the glass vibrating. The movements of the air particles corresponding to the fundamental frequency of 523 cps. will alternately reinforce and oppose these movements, and will do just as much of one as of the other. Nor will the higher harmonics have any appreciable adverse effect. Consequently the glass will be set vibrating with its own frequency, which is that of the second harmonic.

In previous chapters we saw that a sound consists essentially of variations in air pressure due to small movements of the particles of air, which are in their turn caused by movements of the source of sound. Consequently a diagram of a sound wave, such as that in figure 5.1, can be regarded as representing either variations in air pressure, or movements of the source of sound. Similarly the corresponding spectrum gives an indication of the components we would have to use to build up the complex wave; and it also provides a description of the natural frequencies of vibration of the source of sound. These are, of

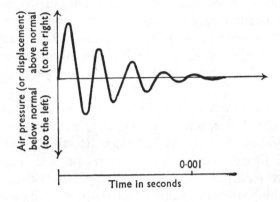

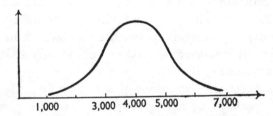

FIG. 5.1. Upper part of figure: a diagram of a sound wave (and of the movements of the source of sound producing the sound wave). Lower part of figure: the spectrum of this sound wave (and of the movements of the source of sound).

course, the frequencies to which the source of sound will respond when it is acting as a resonator. So we see that figure 5.1 can be regarded in two ways: it shows not only the composition of the complex wave emitted by the body, but also the frequencies at which it resonates most easily. In this case the body would respond best to frequencies around 4,000 cps.

(which is the basic component in the complex wave); it would be slightly affected by frequencies around 3,000 and 5,000 cps. (regions in which there are somewhat smaller components in the complex wave); but it would hardly respond at all to frequencies above 7,000 cps. and below 1,000 cps. (regions in which there is scarcely any energy in the complex wave). This principle applies to all sources of sounds. The spectra of the sounds they emit when undergoing free vibrations is also an indication of the frequencies to which the body will respond.

As a further example of this phenomenon we may consider a tuning fork, whose spectrum is a sharply peaked curve. As we saw in the last chapter, this indicates that all the energy is concentrated in one narrow frequency region, i.e. it is very nearly a pure tone. Consequently a tuning fork will resonate only to a sound wave containing this frequency. As we also saw, it is characteristic of a sharply peaked spectrum that it should indicate a source of sound which takes a long time to decay. Equally well, when the tuning fork is acting as a resonator—perhaps resonating to another tuning fork in the way we have already discussed—it takes a comparatively long time for its vibrations to build up.

If we make the vibrations of a tuning fork die away more quickly, perhaps by lightly touching it with a piece of cotton wool, we alter the quality of the sound wave that it produces. In addition we alter the way in which it will respond when it is acting as a resonator. We saw at the end of Chapter 4 that sounds with a more rapid rate of decay have their energy dispersed among a greater range of frequencies. A tuning fork whose vibrations are being made to decay more rapidly will produce a complex wave with a number of component frequencies. Equally well, it will resonate when it is in the presence of any of these frequencies.

A source of sound whose vibrations die away quickly is said to be *damped*. A non-repetitive wave form which decays very rapidly is called a highly damped sound. The sounding board of a piano, and the body of a violin, are examples of damped resonators. Tuning forks are, for practical purposes, undamped sources of sound (although, theoretically, the slight air resistance and other frictional forces, which eventually do slow them down, might be classified as damping forces).

We can now restate our conclusions about resonators in a different form, viz.: damped resonators, whose vibrations build up and die away quickly, can be set in motion by a wide range of frequencies, i.e. they are described by flat curves. Undamped resonators, on the other hand, require a longer time for their vibrations to build up and to die away; they can be set in motion by a limited range of frequencies only, i.e. they are described by sharply peaked curves.

The curve describing the way in which a resonator will vibrate in response to any given frequency is called the *resonance curve*. So that we can see the sort of information conveyed by these curves, we may consider the case of a slightly damped resonator, whose curve is shown in figure 5.2. (This curve, of course, is also a description of the complex wave which would be produced by the resonator.) Now let us suppose that we sound three pure tones, with frequencies of 250 cps., 300 cps., and 375 cps., but all with the same amplitude (i.e. all having peaks of excess pressure of the same size). The resonator will be set in vibration by each of these tones. But it prefers to vibrate at a frequency of 300 cps. Consequently the 300 cps. tone will cause the largest vibrations; the size (or amplitude) of the vibrations which the resonator will make in response to this tone can be represented by the line *b*. Although the 250 cps. tone has the same amplitude as the 300 cps. tone, it will not cause such large vibrations, since this is not the preferred frequency of the resonator; when the resonator is set in motion by the 250 cps. tone it will vibrate with an amplitude represented by the line *a*, i.e. in proportion to the size of the 250 cps. tone in its complex wave. Similarly we can de-

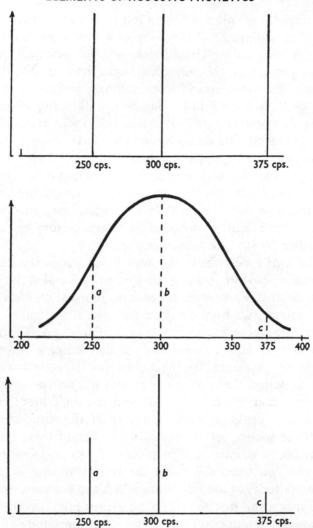

FIG. 5.2. When three pure tones with frequencies and amplitudes as shown in the upper part of the figure are applied separately to a system which has a resonance curve as shown in the middle part of the figure, then the system will vibrate with the frequencies and amplitudes shown in the lower part of the figure.

duce from the curve the size of the vibrations which the resonator will make when it is set in motion by the 375 cps. tone. The resonator has hardly any natural tendency to vibrate at this frequency—the 375 cps. component in its complex wave has a very small amplitude. Consequently a 375 cps. tone will cause only small vibrations of the resonator, their amplitude being represented by the short line c. The size of the resonator's vibrations at any frequency will depend on the extent to which this frequency is present in its complex wave. This is what is meant by saying that the resonance curve of a body has the same shape as its spectrum.

The resonator whose curve is shown in figure 5.2 can be set in vibration effectively by tones with frequencies from about 250 cps. to about 350 cps. Compared with this, the resonance curve shown in figure 5.1 designates a resonator which will respond effectively to a much wider range of frequencies— from somewhere around 3,000 cps. to about 5,000 cps. It is often necessary in acoustics to specify the range of frequencies which can cause a resonator to vibrate. You can, if you like, regard this as a kind of measure of the sensitivity of a resonator. A tuning fork is sensitive to a very narrow range of frequencies, whereas a damped resonator can be set in motion by a much wider range. But it is difficult to give a precise specification of the band of frequencies which can be used to set a resonator in vibration, because of the way in which resonance curves taper away. The resonator discussed in the previous paragraph, for instance, can be set in motion by frequencies of 375 cps. and over; but its vibrations in response to frequencies in this range will be very small, and can be discounted for most practical purposes.

The sounds which we use to try to set a resonator in motion are known as the *input* to the resonator. The way in which the resonator vibrates in response to these sounds is known as its *output* for a given input. Now suppose that the input to a resonator consists of a very large number of tones, all with equal

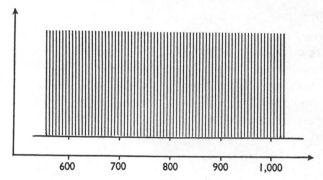

FIG. 5.3. The spectrum of a sound consisting of a large
number of tones with the same amplitude.

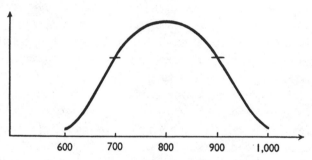

FIG. 5.4. A curve specifying a resonator.

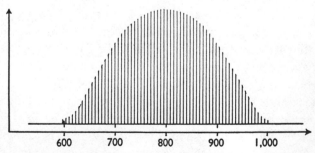

FIG. 5.5. The output of the resonator in fig. 5.4 when
the input shown in fig. 5.3 is applied to it.

amplitudes. Such an input can be represented by the spectrum in figure 5.3. If the resonator in question has a curve with a peak of 800 cps. as shown in figure 5.4, its output will be a sound with the spectrum shown in figure 5.5. It will resonate with maximum efficiency to the 800 cps. tone (which is known as the *resonant frequency*), and with decreasing efficiency to tones on either side of that frequency.

One conventional way of stating the frequency range within which a resonator will respond effectively is to consider the frequencies at which the amplitude of the output is 70·7%* of the output at the resonant frequency. For the resonator in question the outputs at 700 cps. and at 900 cps. will be 70·7% of the output at 800 cps., although the inputs at these three frequencies were all the same. Accordingly we may consider this resonator to be effective within this range. Any frequency between 700 cps. and 900 cps. will set up vibrations whose amplitude will be at least 0·707 of the amplitude of the vibrations caused by an 800 cps. tone of equal strength.

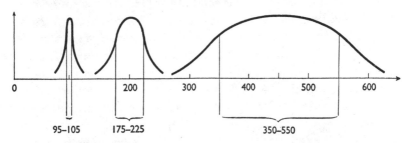

FIG. 5.6. Curves specifying three different resonators, each with a different centre frequency and a different bandwidth.

The effective frequency range of a resonator is known as its *bandwidth*. Diagrams of resonators with bandwidths of 10 cycles (from 95 to 105 cps.), 50 cycles (from 175 to 225 cps.) and 200 cycles (from 350 to 550 cps.) are shown in figure 5.6. As you can see, the peaks of the resonance curves are at 100

* The reason why this particular value is given will appear later, see page 84.

cps., 200 cps., and 450 cps.; frequencies up to 5 cycles, 25 cycles, and 100 cycles on either side of these peaks will produce outputs with at least 70·7% of the amplitude of the output at the resonant frequency.

When we analyse sounds we often use resonators to tell us which frequencies are present. In practice we use electric resonators, which work on similar principles to the tuning forks that we have been considering. If a tuning fork resonated even slightly when a sound occurred, we would know that there was a component with a similar frequency in the complex wave. Electric resonators enable us to perform this kind of analysis with great sensitivity.

There is, however, a difficulty in designing resonators for this purpose. As we have often stressed, resonators with a narrow bandwidth (i.e. with sharply peaked resonance curves) respond to a small range of frequencies, but they take a comparatively long time for the amplitude of their vibrations to build up and they also have a slower rate of decay. They may tell us precisely what frequencies are present in a sound wave, but they take a certain amount of time to do it. Conversely, resonators which will respond to a broad range of frequencies build up to their maximum amplitude far more quickly. They may not tell us the precise frequency of a component of a complex wave, but they need less time to convey the information.

It is because of this that there is a problem in designing a resonator which will respond to a given frequency. Let us suppose, for example, that we wanted to know whether there was a component with a frequency of 500 cps. in a certain speech sound. A resonator which was sensitive to a narrow band of frequencies around 500 cps. would take a certain amount of time for its response to occur. But the speech sound in question might not last that long. Consequently we should have to use a resonator which responded more quickly, which of course means that it also responds to a wider range of frequencies. We can tell the precise frequencies that are present in a sound

only if we have sufficient time for a resonator with a small
bandwidth to be set in vibration.

The length of time which a resonator takes to build up to
a conventional proportion of its full amplitude of vibration is
known as the *time constant* of that resonator. There is actually a
simple mathematical relationship between the bandwidth of
a resonator, and its time constant. In one way of specifying the
time constant, the product of the bandwidth of the resonator
(in cycles) and the time constant (in seconds) equals one half.
Thus if a resonator has a bandwidth of 10 cycles it can be said
to have a time constant of one twentieth of a second, since
$10 \times 1/20 = 1/2$. This means that if we wish to know with
any accuracy whether a given sound contains a component with
a certain frequency, say, 500 cps., and we use a resonator which
responds to a band of frequencies 10 cycles wide—from 495
to 505 cps.—then we must allow at least one twentieth of a
second for the resonator to make a response. But if it is a speech
sound which we are examining, it may change appreciably
in that time; so we may prefer to use a resonator which has a
bandwidth of 50 cycles. This resonator takes $1/50 \times 1/2$ (i.e.
one hundredth of a second) to build up to a comparable
amplitude of vibration. So if we are satisfied with a resonator
which will respond to all frequencies between, for instance,
475 and 525 cps. then we need allow only one hundredth of a
second for it to make its response. With this resonator we could
not tell the precise frequency components of a sound; but we
would be able to get some information during the short time
that the sound lasts.

Most of the resonators with which we have been concerned
have been vibrating bodies, such as tuning forks, and piano
strings. But it is also possible for a body of air to vibrate, and
hence to act as a source of sound or a resonator. This is what
happens when a bottle is made to sound by blowing across the
top of it. The human voice, the organ, and many other instruments make use of a vibrating air column.

When we were considering the transmission of sound in Chapter 1, we saw that air could become compressed and rarefied. If it is suitably contained it can, in fact, behave in a similar way to a coiled spring. A spring can be made to vibrate by giving it a light tap; the rate of the vibrations will be dependent mainly on the size and stiffness of the spring. Similarly, the air in a tube can be set vibrating if it is suitably excited. The rate at which a body of air will vibrate depends upon its size and its elasticity (the factor corresponding to the stiffness of the coiled spring). Normally the elasticity can be regarded as a fixed physical constant; but the size of a body of air can, of course, be altered. As in the case of the coiled spring, a large body of air vibrates more slowly than a small body of air contained in a similar way.

Figure 5.7 shows a typical laboratory arrangement for producing a vibrating column of air. The effective length of the tube can be adjusted by increasing or decreasing the amount of water it contains. When the length is such that the natural rate of vibration of the body of air is the same as that of a tuning fork which is held above it, resonance will occur. Just as in the other examples of resonance, small movements of the tuning fork will act as a series of blows which will eventually build up large movements of the body of air. This movement will cause a disturbance in the surrounding air, which will, of course, spread outwards in the form of sound waves.

The air in a container usually vibrates in a complex manner. Among the factors which influence the form of the complex wave are the shape of the container, and the material of which it is made. For example, a bottle with a thin neck and a large body has a lower fundamental frequency than a stout necked bottle somewhat smaller in size. Resonating air columns are of great importance from our point of view because the differences between many speech sounds are due to the varying shape of the body of air contained in the mouth and throat.

If we sound a whole series of tuning forks above an empty

pipe, some will have no effect at all, whereas others will set the air inside it vibrating. Now let us suppose that this pipe went through a wall. Then when some tuning forks were sounded alongside the pipe, a listener in the other room would hear nothing, others he would hear slightly, and yet others would be heard quite loudly. The loudness with which he would hear a

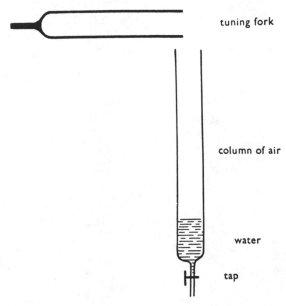

tuning fork

column of air

water

tap

Fig. 5.7. A typical laboratory arrangement for producing a vibrating column of air.

fork would depend on the extent to which the air in the pipe was set in motion by that fork.

When a resonator is behaving in this way we call it an acoustic *filter*. A filter is a resonator which is used to transmit or pass on sound, and which is selective with respect to frequency; in other words, it transmits one frequency with greater efficiency than another. The range of frequencies which a filter will pass on is known as the *bandwidth* of the filter. If the input to a filter consists of a large number of different frequencies, all with the same amplitude, then its bandwidth is said to be the range of frequencies which it will pass on with at least 70·7% of its amplitude of the frequency which it passes with maximum efficiency.

6

Hearing

All students of speech need to be acquainted with some of the facts of hearing. We may begin by considering one or two more points about the perceived pitch of different sounds. In the previous chapters we have presumed that the pitch sensation of a sound is directly dependent on the frequency of the wave. This assumption needs some qualification since a variation in the amplitude of the wave will also affect the pitch sensation. The nature of this effect depends on the frequency of the sound in question. As a rough rule we can say that as the amplitude of any sound with a fundamental frequency above 1,500 cps. increases, so the sound will become not only louder but also higher in pitch. Conversely, if we increase the amplitude of a sound below 1,500 cps. the pitch of the sound will be heard as lower. You can try this effect for yourself by sounding a tuning fork of, say, 200 cps. and moving it backwards and forwards near your ear. When it is close to your ear it will sound not only louder but also slightly lower in pitch than when it is further away. Another way of doing this experiment is to vary the volume control on a radio set while listening to a tuning signal. If the frequency of the tuning signal is below 1,500 cps., then, when you turn the volume control up, the pitch of the sound will be heard as lower. However, as you will see if you try these experiments, variations in amplitude do not have a very great effect on the pitch of a sound, so that for most practical purposes we can still say that the pitch that we hear depends on the frequency of the wave form.

There remains, however, the question of the pitch of complex sounds in which there is energy at more than one frequency. In complex sounds with non-repetitive wave forms the perceived pitch depends on a kind of average of the component frequencies. In a damped wave with a symmetrical spectrum as shown in figure 6.1 the pitch will depend mainly on the frequency of the component with the largest amplitude, which is often called the *basic frequency* of that wave.

On the other hand, the perceived pitch of a complex sound with a repetitive wave form depends not on the frequency of the component with the largest amplitude, but on the fundamental frequency of repetition of the complex wave. For example, the wave form shown in figure 6.2 has a fundamental frequency of 100 cps. Consequently the pitch of this wave form will be the same as that of a pure tone with a frequency of 100 cps., and a comparable amplitude. The fact that the second and third harmonics both have a greater amplitude than that of the fundamental frequency is of no consequence as far as the perceived pitch of the sound is concerned.

It is important to note that, when we make a frequency analysis of a complex wave, we may find that there is no component with a frequency which is the same as the frequency of repetition of the complex wave. If the wave form shown in figure 6.3 continued indefinitely it could be analysed into components with frequencies of 1,800, 2,000, and 2,200 cps. But the complex wave form repeats itself 200 times a second (i.e. from *a* to *b* is 1/200 of a second). Consequently the perceived pitch of this sound will be the same as that of a pure tone with a frequency of 200 c̈ps. although the complex wave can be said to have only an imaginary component with this frequency. (Another way of looking at the frequency analysis of this complex wave is to say that there are components with frequencies of 200, 400, 600, 800, ... and all the other whole number of multiples of 200; but only three of these components (those with frequencies of 1,800, 2,000, and 2,200 cps.) have any amplitude.)

Because the ear detects pitch in this way, we can often remove

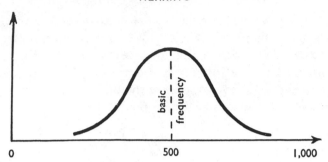

FIG. 6.1. The spectrum of a damped wave.

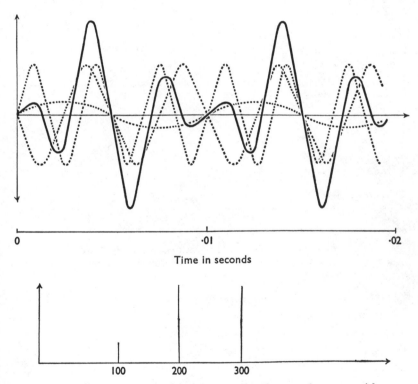

Time in seconds

FIG. 6.2. The wave form and spectrum of a complex wave with a pitch the same as that of a pure tone of 100 cps.

all the lower frequency components in a complex wave without affecting the perceived pitch. We could, for example, pass a complex wave with a fundamental frequency of 100 cps. through an electrical filter which cuts out all the frequencies below 500 cps. As long as some of the higher frequencies components are still separated from one another by 100 cps., the

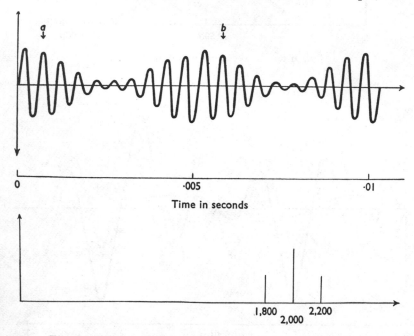

Fig. 6.3. The wave form and spectrum of a complex wave with a pitch the same as that of a pure tone of 200 cps.

complex wave will still be repeated 100 times a second, and the pitch that we hear will be unaltered. In fact an ordinary telephone circuit does not pass much energy below 300 cps. Although this will affect the quality of the sound (since the quality depends on the way in which the energy is distributed among the frequency components), nevertheless the perceived pitch will remain the same.

This difference between the ways in which the ear detects different aspects of a sound affects the kind of analysis we make. When we want to compare the different qualities of two sounds, an analysis in terms of the frequency components will enable us to make the simplest statements, and diagrams of the spectra will be the most useful form of presentation of the data in visual terms. But when we want to consider differences in pitch that we hear, we are concerned with the fundamental frequencies; in such cases diagrams of the complex waves are usually sufficient in themselves.

In this book we are not concerned with the physiology of hearing. The function of the ear is to turn sound waves, which are an acoustic form of energy, into nerve impulses, which are an electro-chemical form of energy that can be handled within the brain. The way in which this happens is outside our scope. But it is interesting to note that many of the modern theories of hearing consider that the ear produces a pattern of impulses which corresponds to some kind of frequency analysis of the complex wave, and an additional series of impulses corresponding in part to the rate of repetition of the complex wave. In all probability, what we hear as the quality of a sound is largely dependent on the first set of impulses; whereas the perceived pitch (at any rate of low notes) depends on the second.

The ear is capable of distinguishing between a large number of different pitches. The variation in frequency which we can just detect as a change in pitch is about 2 or 3 cps. in notes with frequencies below 1,000 cps. For higher notes an increasingly large change has to be made before we hear any variation in pitch. One set of values for the sensitivity of the ear to changes in frequency is shown in figure 6.4. As you can see, the change in frequency in higher notes that can just be heard as a change in pitch is a more or less constant proportion—about 1/500 or 0.002—of the frequency of the sound. Thus the just noticeable difference in frequency at 4,000 cps. is about 0·002 ×

4,000, i.e. 8 cps.; and at 7,000 it is nearly 0·002 × 7,000, i.e. 14 cps.

Since the ear is more sensitive to changes in frequency in the lower part of the scale, the differences in pitch between notes with frequencies of 600 and 700 cps. will be far greater than the difference between notes of 3,600 and 3,700 cps.

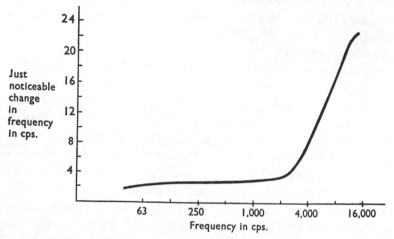

FIG. 6.4. A graph showing how much the frequency of a tone has to be altered in order to produce a change in pitch.

Between the first pair of notes there will be about 35 just noticeable differences in frequency, but between the higher pair there will be only 14. In this region notes must be separated by approximately 250 cps. to make a difference in pitch comparable with the difference between 600 and 700 cps.

We often want to represent a difference in perceived pitch between notes by means of points on a diagram or graph which shows differences in frequency. For many purposes it would be convenient if we could represent equal intervals in pitch by equally spaced points on the graph. To do this we want to know the relation between the frequency of a note and its height on the pitch scale. This relationship has been found by various psychological experiments, all of which show that the ear actually behaves in a very complex way. But as a rough rule we can say that the perceived pitch of a note increases regularly with its frequency between 100 and 1,000 cps., so that, for example, the difference in pitch between notes with frequencies of 300 and 450 cps. is much the same as the differences between notes with frequencies of 450 and 600 cps., and 750 and 900 cps. But between 1,000 and 10,000 cps. the relation between the pitch we hear and the actual frequency of a note is what mathematicians call logarithmic; this means that the pitch interval between two notes in this range depends on the ratio of the two frequencies, so that, for example, from 1,500 to 3,000 cps. (a ratio of 1 to 2) and from 4,000 to 8,000 (also a ratio of 1 to 2) are equal intervals of pitch (although the first pair of notes are separated by 1,500 cps. as compared with the 4,000 cps. that separate the second pair).

Despite the fact that this rule for the relation between perceived pitch and frequency is only an approximation, it is sufficiently accurate for many purposes. Consequently graph paper has been devised in which the frequency scale is divided in this way. Figure 6.5 shows a piece of this graph paper on which a number of pairs of notes have been plotted. If this rule were exact, each pair of notes would represent precisely the same interval of pitch. Below 1,000 cps. the notes are separated by a constant frequency (250 cps.); but above 1,000 cps. it is the ratio (1 to 1·3) that is fixed. However, all the lines joining these notes are equal in length. The advantage of this sort of graph paper is that at any point a given vertical distance always represents roughly the same change in perceived pitch. This type of scale, which is called the Koenig scale, is often used in acoustic phonetics.

An even more accurate way of representing differences in pitch is by means of the *mel* scale. The mel is defined as the unit of pitch, so that when pairs of sounds are separated by an equal number of mels, they are also separated by equal inter-

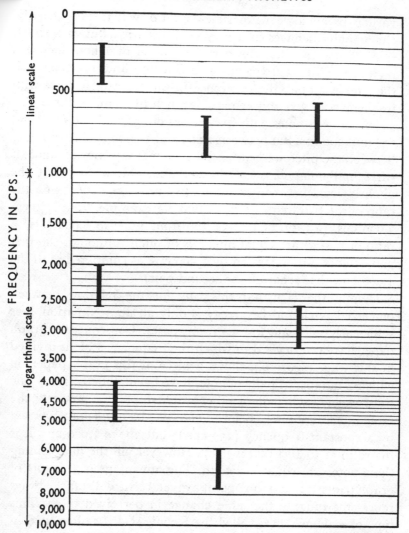

Fig. 6.5. The Koenig scale. The lines represent pairs of notes which are separated by similar intervals of pitch.

vals of pitch. The unit is derived from numerous psycho-physical experiments in which subjects were asked to perform tasks such as deciding when one tone was half the pitch of another, and when one tone was midway in pitch between two others. These experiments enabled a graph to be drawn showing the relation between the frequency of a note and its value on the mel scale. The following table gives you an idea of the mel values of a few frequencies.

Pitch in mels	Frequency in cps.	Pitch in mels	Frequency in cps.
0	20	1,250	1,420
250	160	1,500	1,900
500	394	1,750	2,450
750	670	2,000	3,120
1,000	1,000	2,250	4,000

Frequency data about speech sounds are often converted into mel units before being presented graphically.

We may now turn to an examination of the loudness of different sounds. We have already seen that the loudness of a sound is mainly dependent on the amplitude of the wave. So far we have been using the term amplitude in a general way to indicate any variation above or below normal air pressure. But let us suppose that we wish to compare the amplitudes of the two sounds whose wave forms are shown in figure 6.6. To make a valid comparison we must consider not the maximum amplitudes, but some sort of average of all the variations from normal pressure in each of these two wave forms. Now if we make a straightforward arithmetical average, the result is in each case zero, since every increase is exactly matched by a subsequent decrease in pressure. Consequently it is useful to make use of a mathematical device which gives us another form of average, known as the r.m.s. value, which is more in keeping with our common-sense ideas about the average amplitudes of these two wave forms. If you are not particularly good at mathematics you can simply regard the r.m.s. amplitude as a useful form of average of the variations in pressure in a sound, and not worry about the details of the method. In actual fact r.m.s. stands for root-mean-square, and the way in which we arrive at this quantity is to square the values of all the points through which the line passes (which turns them all into positive values, since e.g. —2 times —2 equals +4), then take the mean (or average) of these values, and then take the square root of this quantity. This value is a measure of the average variation in air pressure. The r.m.s. values of the amplitudes of the waves shown in figure 6.6 are indicated by means of a

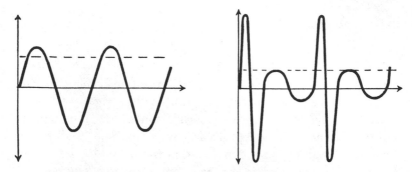

Fig. 6.6. Two complex waves. When comparing the loudness of these two sounds we must consider the r.m.s. amplitudes (shown by dashed lines) rather than the peak amplitudes.

dashed line. In the case of these two waves, the one which has the smaller peak amplitude (i.e. the smaller maximum variation in air pressure) has the larger r.m.s. amplitude. Since the loudness of a sound depends on the r.m.s. amplitude and not on the peak amplitude, the first sound is louder than the second.

As long as we are concerned simply with stating whether one sound is louder than another, then we need know only whether the amplitude of the one is greater than the amplitude of the other. But if we want to say *how much* louder the one sound is, we must compare the *power* of the two sounds. The power of a sound depends on the square of the amplitude. Thus, if the amplitude of a sound is doubled, the power is increased by a

factor of two squared, i.e. by four; and if the amplitude is the
trebled, the power is increased nine-fold, so that it is thirty-
six times its original value. As we shall see, the differences in
power between sounds are often enormous.

The actual value of the power of a sound can be precisely
specified in the units used by physicists. Similarly the amplitude
can be stated in terms of the units which physicists use in their
measurements of air pressure. However we need not worry
about the nature of these units, since we are usually concerned
not with the absolute values of the power or the amplitude of a
sound, but only their value in relation to other sounds. A
common practice is to define as a reference level a sound
which has an amplitude of 0·0002 dynes per square centimetre, and a power of 10^{-16} watts per square centimetre.
Once we have done this we can consider the amplitude or the
power of any sound as being so much larger or so much smaller
than that of the reference sound.

The reference sound which we have defined is one which is
not quite as loud as the quietest sound that can just be heard
under suitable experimental conditions. The loudest sound that
we can stand without a feeling of pain in our ears has more
than 1,000,000,000,000 times more power than this (which
means, of course, that its amplitude is over 1,000,000 times
greater than that of the reference sound).

Figure 6.7 shows the powers of sounds constituting thirteen
approximately equal steps of loudness, starting from the reference
level and going up to the loudest note we can stand without
a feeling of pain. As you can see, the difference in power (in
actual watts per square centimetre) is far greater between steps
twelve and thirteen than it is between steps one and two, or
two and three: but the power ratio between any two adjacent
steps remains the same.

It is partly because the differences in power among sounds
are so large, and partly because the differences in loudness
depend on the ratio of the powers rather than on the actual

alues, that acousticians have adopted the decibel scale. The difference in decibels between two sounds is defined as ten times the common logarithm of their power ratios. This is not actually as complicated as it appears, and should prove to be understandable even by those who have forgotten what is meant by a common logarithm. The following table will help to make the matter clearer.

Power ratio between sounds	Common logarithm of the power ratio	Difference in decibels
10 to 1	1	10
100 to 1	2	20
1,000 to 1	3	30

As you can see, all you have to do to find the common logarithm of the power ratios shown in the table is to count the number of noughts. The difference in decibels between the two sounds can then be found by multiplying this number by ten. If we apply this method to the power ratios shown in figure 6.7, we find that the common logarithm of the power ratio between the greatest sound that the human ear can stand and the reference level is thirteen, since this number has thirteen noughts in it. The difference in decibels (or db to use the common abbreviation) between these two sounds is therefore ten times this, i.e. 130 db. Similarly the difference in db between, for example, steps three and five is twenty db, since the power at step five is 100 times greater than it is at step three, and the common logarithm of 100 is two. This is, of course, the same as the difference between steps six and eight, or any other pair of steps which have a power ratio of 100 to 1.

By now you can probably see the advantages of using the decibel scale. Each step in figure 6.7 corresponds (roughly) to an equal increment in loudness. The differences in power vary immensely. But when these differences are stated in decibels, each step is seen to be the same. By means of the decibel system, not only are the awkward numbers involved reduced to manageable proportions, but also differences in power between sounds are stated in a way which corresponds very nearly with our ideas of loudness. There is at the most a 10% error involved in equating our impressions of differences

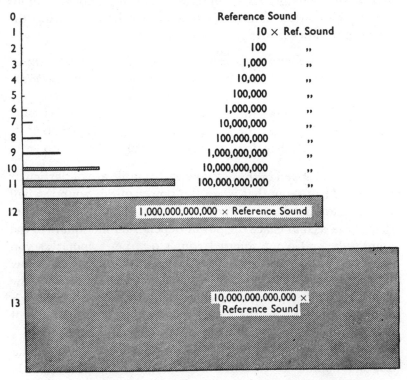

FIG. 6.7. The powers of sounds constituting thirteen approximately equal steps of loudness. The power of each sound in watts per sq. cm. is proportional to the *area* of each block.

in loudness with the actual differences in decibels between sounds.

Of course, the rule we have given for finding the common logarithm of a number applies only to figures of the form 10, or 100, or 1,000, etc. When the power ratio between two sounds is some intermediate value, such as 67 to 1, we have to use logarithm tables as a step in finding the differences in decibels between the sounds. The following table gives you some idea of a few of these intermediate values. Since, in the earlier part of this book, we talked in terms of the amplitudes of sounds rather than in terms of their powers, a column showing the amplitude ratios is also included.

Amplitude ratio between sounds	Power ratio between sounds	Log. of the power ratio	Difference in decibels
0·707	0·5 (or 1 to 2)	0.3	3
0·50	0·25 (or 1 to 4)	0.6	6
0·32	0·10 (or 1 to 10)	1.0	10

The values given in the first row of this table are of particular interest. They show that when the power of one sound is half that of another, the amplitude of the first sound is 0·707 times that of the second (since the power depends on the square of the amplitude, and 0·707 squared equals 0·5, i.e. a half); as you can see, under these circumstances the one sound is 3 db below the other. These values are important because, as we saw earlier (page 65), we usually consider the effective bandwidth of a resonator to be the range over which a resonator will respond to a level input in such a way that all the frequencies within this range have an amplitude of at least 70·7% of the largest amplitude. Now that the connection between amplitude and power has been explained, we can see how the value 70·7% arises; all the frequencies within this range have at least half the power of the maximum output. Accordingly this measure of the effective range of a resonator is often known as the half-power bandwidth.

At the beginning of the section on amplitude and power we said that the reference sound was almost as loud as the softest sound that the ear could just detect under suitable experimental conditions. In fact the power that a sound has to have before we can hear it depends on the frequency of the sound. We can hear notes in the middle of the frequency range when they are only a little more powerful than the reference sound; but very low notes or very high notes have to be far more powerful before we can hear them. The lower curve in figure 6.8 shows the range of values applicable to a young per-

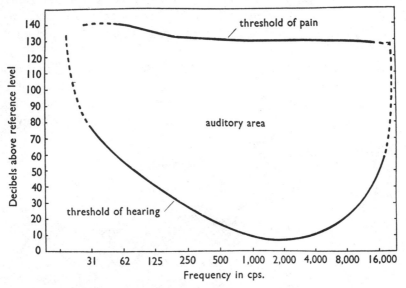

FIG. 6.8. A graph in which the auditory area shows the frequency and amplitude limits of all audible tones.

son with normal hearing. As you can see, when a tone with a frequency of 125 cps. is just audible, it is 30 db more powerful than the just audible note with a frequency of 2,000 cps. In other words the ear is more efficient in the middle of its range. It takes a good deal more power to make it work either for very low notes or for very high notes. Once we get beyond certain frequency limits there cannot be a sensation of sound, no matter how great the power of the disturbance in the air may be. This is probably because some part of the mechanism of the ear cannot be made to vibrate at these extremely high or low frequencies.

The upper line in figure 6.8 represents the level at which the sounds begin to cause a feeling of pain in the ear. If the power of a sound of almost any frequency is raised until it is 130 db above the reference level, then there will be a feeling of discomfort. Accordingly figure 6.8 shows the total extent of possible auditory sensations; all audible variations in air pressure must have frequencies and amplitudes which lie within the ranges indicated.

So far in this chapter we have said nothing about differences in quality among sounds. This is largely because we can usually discuss the quality of a sound in terms of the frequencies and amplitudes of its components, i.e. in terms of its spectrum.

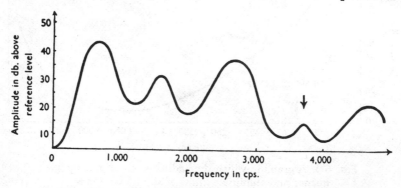

FIG. 6.9. The spectrum of a complex sound in which the components in the peak marked with an arrow are masked by the other components with greater amplitude.

There are, however, one or two additional factors which we must take into account. The most important of these is a phenomenon which is known as *masking*. One sound is said to be masked by a second sound when it cannot be heard because of the presence of the other sound. Most of the work on this topic has been done using pure tones rather than complex sounds such as those of speech. But the work that has been done shows

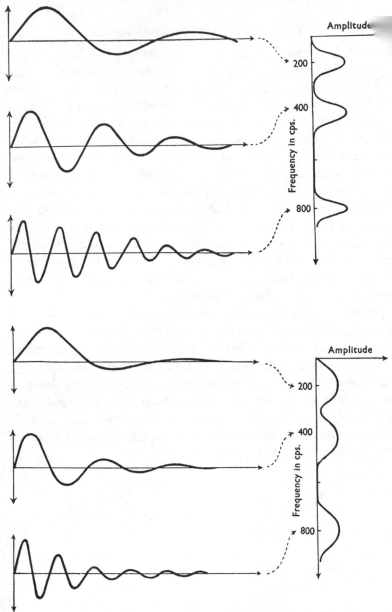

FIG. 6.10. Two sounds each composed of three damped waves. The peaks in the spectrum of the sound in the lower part of the figure are broader than those of the sound in the upper part of the figure; and the components in the lower part of the figure are correspondingly more highly damped. There is very little auditory difference between these two sounds.

that if, for instance, the amplitude of a pure tone with a frequency of 3,500 cps. is 40 db below the amplitude of a tone with a frequency of 2,500 cps., then the 3,500 cps. tone will not be heard because it is masked by the other tone. This kind of work is very important in our consideration of the perception of speech sounds. It shows that in a sound such as that shown in figure 6.9, the peak marked ↓ is insignificant from the listener's point of view because it probably cannot be heard in the presence of the other components with greater amplitudes. Unfortunately there has not been enough research on this problem for us to be able to say with any certainty which of the other minor peaks we can disregard, and which add something to the total quality. Further research on the masking of complex sounds would be of great assistance to us in our evaluation of the spectra of speech sounds.

Further research is also needed in connection with our perception of damped wave forms. There is much that we do not know about the effect of different degrees of damping. There is every indication that there is very little apparent difference between a sound consisting of three lightly damped waves as in the upper part of figure 6.10 and the sound composed of three heavily damped waves shown immediately below it. But it is not possible to say much about the limits of this phenomenon at the moment.

7

The Production of Speech

When we talk we use our tongues and lips and other vocal organs to produce the different speech sounds. Many of the books on speech give accounts of the positions of the vocal organs which accompany these different sounds; but, with one or two exceptions, there has been little attempt to show how the movements of the vocal organs actually generate the variations in air pressure which are peculiar to each speech sound. It is not within the scope of this book to give a detailed explanation of all the various sounds of speech. But in this chapter the method of producing each of the main types of sounds that occur in English is considered.

At the beginning of this book we pointed out that for every sound there must be a corresponding movement of a source of sound. In the majority of speech sounds the vibrations of the air in the passages of the mouth, throat, and nose (which are collectively known as the vocal tract) serve as the movements which initiate the sound waves. The vocal tract is terminated at one end by the vocal cords and at the other is open to the air beyond the lips and nostrils; thus it forms a resonating chamber of a complex shape. When the air in this chamber is set in motion by a sharp tap it vibrates in a complex way; it is these vibrations that cause the sound waves which we hear.

The taps that set the air in the mouth and throat in vibration are due to the action of the vocal cords on the air which is being forced out of the lungs. The air in the lungs is compressed due to the action of the respiratory muscles. When the vocal cords, which are actually small folds of muscle and cartilage in the larynx, are together pressure is built up beneath them. If this pressure is big enough, the vocal cords may be forced apart and the lung air released. This sudden release of air under pressure acts like a sharp tap on the air in the vocal tract, which is accordingly set vibrating.

The air in the vocal tract will, of course, vibrate in different ways when the vocal organs are in different positions. As we stated in Chapter 5, the way in which a body of air vibrates depends on its size and shape. The variations in the shape of the vocal tract are determined largely by the movements of the tongue, the lips, and the soft palate. There will be a characteristic mode of vibration of the air corresponding to each position of these vocal organs.

We can now see how the wave forms of the vowel sounds which we discussed in Chapter 3 were generated. The wave form of the vowel [ɔ] as in *caught* is repeated here in figure 7.1. As we have already noted, it consists of a series of damped waves, recurring on this occasion at the rate of 100 a second. Each of these damped waves is produced by the vibrations of the air in the vocal tract which recur every time there is a pulse from the vocal cords. As long as the vocal organs are in the positions for this vowel, and the vocal cords continue producing pulses, a series of damped waves of this kind will be generated.

When the vocal organs take up another position, such as that for the vowel [i] in *see*, another series of damped waves is produced. As we can see from figure 7.2, which is a repetition of another part of figure 3.3, the wave form has at least two principal components which are distinguishable by eye. In fact it would be better to consider the wave form for [i] *see* as being more like the sum of three damped waves; and even this is a simplification, as there are some additional smaller components. Damped waves with appropriate frequencies are shown in figure 7.3. Every time there is a pulse from the vocal cords the air in the mouth and throat is set vibrating in all

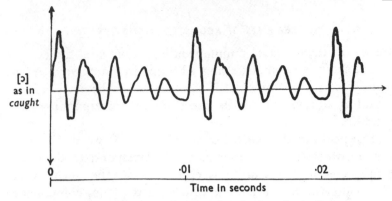

FIG. 7.1. The wave form produced when the author
pronounced the vowel [ɔ] as in *caught*.

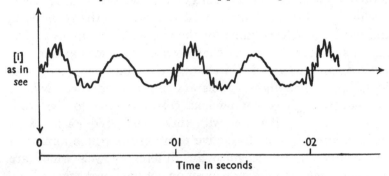

FIG. 7.2. The wave form produced when the author
pronounced the vowel [i] as in *see*.

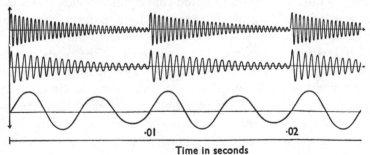

FIG. 7.3. Three damped waves (the top one with a basic
frequency of 3,500 cps., the middle one with a basic frequency
of 2,200 cps., and the lower one with a basic frequency of 200
cps.) each with a fundamental frequency of 100 cps. If these
three wave forms were added together they would produce a
sound wave very like that of [i] as in *see*.

three of these ways simultaneously. (Compare figure 3.2 which shows a stretched string vibrating in many ways at the same time.) The sound [i] is the sum of all these vibrations, and has components in its spectrum at corresponding frequencies.

The peaks in the spectra of vowels (and, as we shall see, of certain other speech sounds as well) correspond to the basic frequencies of the vibrations of the air in the vocal tract. The regions of the spectrum in which the frequency components are relatively large (i.e. the regions around these peaks) are known as *formants*. The formants of a sound are thus aspects of it which are directly dependent on the shape of the vocal tract, and are largely responsible for the characteristic quality. The author's vowel [ɔ] is partly characterized by a formant around 500 cps., and his vowel [i] by formants around 220, 2,300, and 3,500 cps. When these vowels are pronounced there will be comparatively large components corresponding to the components of damped waves with these basic frequencies. It is the presence of these distinctive components (these formants) that enables us to recognize the different vowels which are associated with the different positions of the vocal organs.

So far we have not considered the action of the vocal cords in any detail; we have only noted that a pulse occurs when the pressure of the lung air is great enough to force the vocal cords apart. In many speech sounds (such as the vowels [ɔ] and [i] which we have been considering) the vocal cords usually produce a series of pulses: as soon as the cords have been forced apart some lung air escapes; this flow of air actually helps draw the vocal cords together again; when they are together the pressure will once more be built up until the lung air can blow the cords apart again, whereupon the cycle continues as before.

It is important to realize that the movements of the vocal cords are not themselves sufficient to set up vibrations which will be heard as sounds. But whenever the vocal cords are blown apart the released pressure acts like a sharp tap on the air contained in the vocal tract. Each of these taps sets the body of air above the vocal cords vibrating at its own natural frequencies (the formant frequencies). If the vocal cords are blown apart every hundredth of a second, the damped vibrations will be initiated a hundred times a second, and the complex wave form which is produced beyond the lips will be repeated at the same rate. This point is illustrated in figure 7.4, which shows the sound waves corresponding to an electrically synthesized sound that has a slightly simpler wave form, but is almost indistinguishable from the vowel [ɔ] as in *caught* (a) as a result of a single pulse, (b) as the result of pulses recurring every hundredth of a second, (c) and (d) as the result of pulses at two other rates. (An artificial speech synthesizer was used to produce the sounds for these diagrams so as to ensure that the only difference between the sounds was the rate at which the pulses were produced.)

We saw in Chapter 4 that repetitive wave forms such as that in figure 7.4(b) can be conveniently regarded as being the sum of a number of components, each of which has a frequency that is a whole number multiple of the fundamental frequency (i.e. the frequency of repetition of the complex wave). Thus the wave in figure 7.4(b) will have components that are whole number multiples of 100, since this complex wave is repeated 100 times a second. In fact the spectrum of this sound is as shown on the right of the figure. The component with a frequency of 500 cps. has the largest amplitude (which is not surprising, since the damped wave that is repeated has a basic frequency of 500 cps.). In addition there is another peak in the spectrum at 1,500 cps., which corresponds to the smaller waves superimposed on the main damped wave form. In (c) and (d) of figure 7.4 are the wave forms and spectra of the same vowel-like sound on a higher pitch, i.e. when the pulses are being produced at 120 and 150 cps. As you can see, these waves all consist of repetitions of a damped wave with a basic

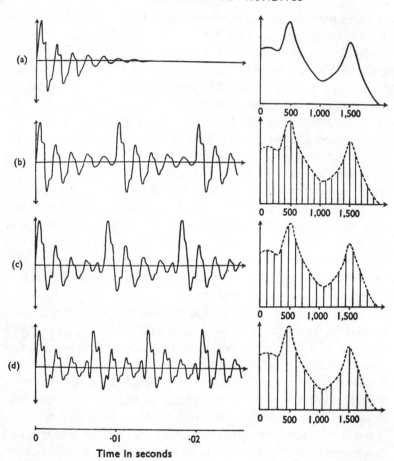

FIG. 7.4. Wave forms and spectra for a synthetic vowel similar to the vowel [ɔ] as in *caught*. (a) Effect of a single pulse on the resonating system; (b) pulses recurring at the rate of 100 a second; (c) 120 pulses a second; (d) 150 pulses a second.

frequency of 500 cps. and another wave with a basic frequency of about 1,500 cps. Furthermore, all the spectra shown on the right of the figure have a certain similarity to one another; it is possible to draw a curve with peaks at 500 and 1,500 cps.

round all of them. The difference between these last two spectra is that the component frequencies are multiples in the one case of 120, and in the other of 150; and hence they are represented by lines which are farther apart.

This analysis is, of course, in accordance with the principle stated in Chapter 4 (pages 51–54): when a complex wave consists of a damped wave form repeated at regular intervals, the component frequencies will always have the same relative amplitudes as the corresponding components in the continuous spectrum representing the isolated occurrence of the damped wave. Consequently, altering the rate at which the vocal cords produce pulses will affect the fundamental frequency of the complex wave; but it will not alter the formants (the peaks in the spectrum), which correspond to the basic frequencies of the damped vibrations of the air in the vocal tract. It is in this sense that we may say that the formants of a sound are properties of the corresponding mouth shape.

Since a continuous curve as in figure 7.4(a) is the clearest way of representing the formants which characterize a given vowel irrespective of the rate at which pulses are produced by the vocal cords, we shall often use it in preference to a line spectrum when we are discussing the acoustic nature of vowel quality. We shall describe a vowel in terms of line spectra (as in figure 7.4(b), (c) and (d)) only when we want to draw attention to the particular fundamental frequencies employed.

We saw in Chapter 6 that the pitch of a sound depends mainly on the fundamental frequency. Accordingly, when there is a variation in the rate at which pulses are produced by the vocal cords, there will be a change in the pitch of the sound (although there will be no change in the formants, and hence no change in the characteristic vowel quality). We control changes in pitch by adjusting the muscles that act upon the cords. When the tension is increased so that the cords are tightly stretched, they move more rapidly, and so produce the greater number of pulses per second that are required for

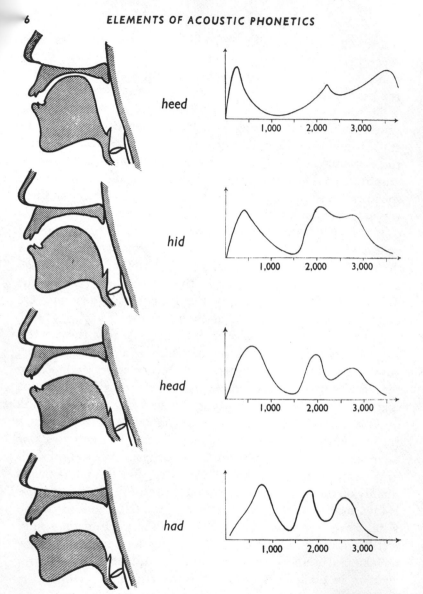

FIG. 7.5. The positions of the vocal organs (based on data from sounds in the middle of the words *heed, hid, head,*

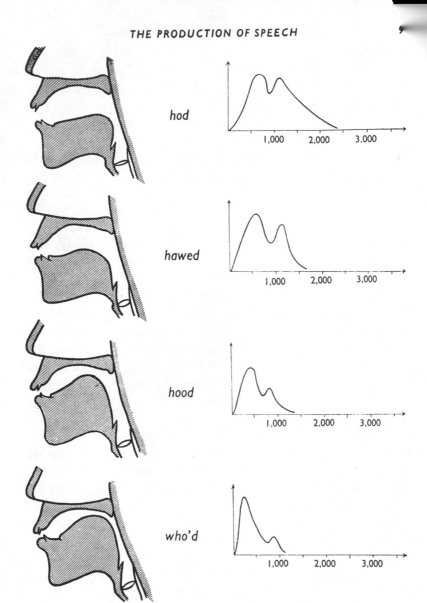

X-ray photographs of the author) and the spectra of the vowel
had, hod, hawed, hood, who'd in the author's speech.

a high pitched sound. On the other hand, in saying a word on a low pitch, the cords are only loosely held together, so that when they have been blown apart they take somewhat longer to return to the closed position.

It is usually possible to alter the pitch of a vowel sound without altering its characteristic quality, because each of these factors is controlled by a separate physiological mechanism: as we have seen, the pitch depends on the action of the vocal cords, and the characteristic quality depends largely on the formants, which have certain fixed values for each particular shape of the vocal tract. Figure 7.5 shows the spectra of the author's vowels in the middle parts of the words *heed, hid, head, had, hod, hawed, hood,* and *who'd*: the corresponding positions of the vocal organs are also shown. These curves give a very good indication of the frequency components which are characteristic of each of these sounds. We may think of each peak as showing the basic frequency of one of the damped waves which are present. The vowel in the middle part of the word *had,* for instance, is characterized by having components with relatively large amplitudes in three main regions: around 700 cps., 1,750 cps., and 2,600 cps. Damped waves with these basic frequencies are generated every time there is a pulse from the vocal cords.

If you like to think of it in musical terms, you can say that corresponding to each vowel there is a chord that is characteristic of that vowel. Owing to the pulses from the larynx, this chord is generated many times a second. There is, of course, nothing particularly new about this way of looking at speech sounds. As long ago as 1829 Robert Willis said: "A given vowel is merely the rapid repetition of its peculiar note." This is an over-simplification, because Willis did not realize that many vowels are characterized not by one frequency each, but by a combination of frequencies; but if we alter his remark slightly, and say that a given vowel is merely the rapid repetition of its peculiar *chord,* we have a statement that fits the data of figure 7.5 very nicely.

There are, of course, other possible ways of describing the production of vowel sounds. One popular method, which was used by Martin Joos in his excellent monograph *Acoustic Phonetics* (see annotated bibliography), regards the pulse produced by the vocal cords as a wave which is affected by having to pass through the vocal tract. The wave form of the glottal pulse is considered to be as shown in figure 7.6. The spectrum of a wave of this kind consists of a large number of harmonics with decreasing amplitudes. If the wave form were of the more regular form shown in figure 7.7, the spectrum would actually be as shown in figure 7.8. This kind of wave form is regarded as a disturbance which occurs at the vocal cords. It is then said to be modified by the filtering action of the vocal tract, which transmits some harmonics with greater efficiency than others. Consequently the spectrum of the wave form beyond the lips will have peaks in regions which depend on the filter characteristic of the vocal tract. Since the characteristic of the vocal tract depends on its shape, the positions of these peaks are in fact determined by the position of the vocal organs.

This method of describing the production of certain speech sounds has the advantage that it makes it simple to allow for variations in the shape of the pulse produced by the vocal cords. In our account we have been tacitly implying that it is always the same. But in fact it varies greatly from person to person; and these variations will affect the complex wave (though not usually to such an extent that there is a significant difference in the formants that characterize the sounds).

On the other hand, our method of considering the vocal tract as a mechanism for producing damped waves that recur every time there is a pulse from the vocal cords is in many respects a neater way of describing the production of the acoustic elements that characterize vowels and other speech sounds. This method correctly emphasizes that the formant frequencies correspond to the basic frequencies of the vibrations of the air in the vocal tract.

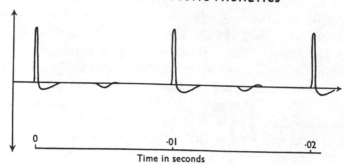

FIG. 7.6. The wave form of the glottal pulse according to Joos. (Recent research has shown that the actual wave form is usually not such a narrow pulse.)

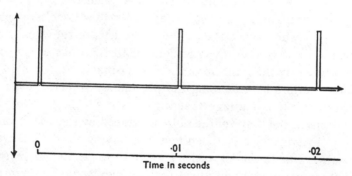

FIG. 7.7. A simplified form of the wave shown in fig. 7.6.

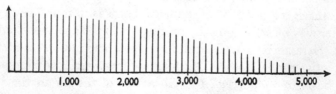

FIG. 7.8. The spectrum of the wave shown in fig. 7.7.

Since vowels are characterized to such an extent by the frequencies of their formants, it is often convenient to represent them by a diagram (figure 7.9) which shows only this information. This diagram, which is based on the data shown in figure 7.5, uses the vertical scale to indicate the frequencies of the formants that characterize the various vowels. It is in some ways similar to the visible picture of speech produced by the sound spectrograph, which is an instrument that automatically analyses sound waves in terms of their component frequencies. This device marks a sheet of special paper in such a way that the horizontal scale of the paper indicates the time at which a certain sound occurred; the vertical scale indicates the component frequencies that are present at the times shown on the horizontal scale; and the lightness or darkness of the marking indicates the amplitudes of the various components. The use of this instrument is discussed in more detail in the author's forthcoming *Speech in the Laboratory*.

Figure 7.9 is one of the basic diagrams in the study of the acoustics of speech. It is, as we have said, derived from the curves shown in figure 7.5, which were actually obtained with the aid of a sound spectrograph. But we can nevertheless verify some of these data without using any instruments. It is, for instance, possible to set the air in the vocal tract vibrating in such a way that the damped wave corresponding to the lowest formant is produced with a greater amplitude than the other components. This can be done by flicking a finger against the throat just above the larynx whilst holding the breath by means of a glottal stop (the sound used by cockney and other dialect speakers in the middle of the word *bottle*). When you do this a dull hollow note is produced. This sound is mainly composed of a damped wave with a basic frequency corresponding to that of the first formant.

If you look at figure 7.9 you will see that the first formant (i.e. the lowest peak in the spectrum) is at a low frequency for the word *heed* (220 cps.) and is a little higher for each of the words *hid* (400 cps.), *head* (550 cps.) and *had* (750 cps.). If you place your vocal organs in the positions for making the vowels in each of these words and then flick your finger against your throat while holding a glottal stop, you will produce a low pitched note for the word *heed*, and a slightly higher one for each of the words *hid*, *head*, and *had*. In the remaining words in this series the frequency of the first formant descends. Conse-

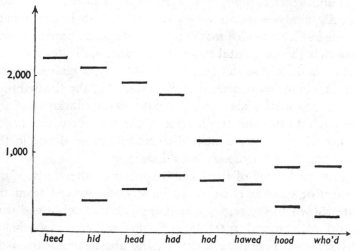

FIG. 7.9. A spectrogram showing the frequencies of the first and second formants of some of the English vowels as pronounced by the author.

quently, if you repeat this trick while making the articulations for the vowels in the words *hod*, *hawed*, *hood*, and *who'd*, you will produce a series of notes which descend in pitch. The actual frequencies of the notes you produce may, of course, differ from those quoted above, which are round values based on an analysis of the author's speech. You may have not only a different accent, but also a differently shaped vocal tract. Both these features will affect the absolute values of the formant frequencies; but they will probably not affect the relative arrangement of the sounds you produce.

We can make a rough check on the frequency of the seco. formant for each of these vowels by whispering the words When you whisper the vocal cords are held slightly apart, so that the air from the lungs rushes through them causing small variations in air pressure which will set the air in the vocal tract vibrating. Among the basic frequencies which are often the most clearly audible under these conditions are those of the second and higher formants. If you whisper the words *heed, hid, head, had, hod, hawed, hood, who'd* you will hear a gradual lowering of the apparent pitch. As you can see from figure 7.9 this is paralleled by the way in which the second formant becomes progressively lower for each of the vowels in this series. It should be noted, however, that this is a very rough method of checking one of the basic frequencies associated with a vowel. When we whisper each of the first four words in the series *heed, hid,* etc., the pitch of the whispered sound probably does correspond more or less to the frequency of the second formant: but for the last four words, when the two peaks are fairly close together, and the amplitude of the lowest one is relatively greater, the whisper pitch may correspond more to the first peak than to the second.

It used to be said that the lowest peak in the spectrum (i.e. the first formant) corresponded to the way in which the air vibrated in the large chamber in the throat behind the highest point of the tongue; whereas the second peak in the spectrum was due to the natural mode of vibration of the air in the mouth in front of the highest point of the tongue. In fact the air in the vocal tract vibrates as a whole, and we cannot treat the throat and mouth cavities as being in any way independent. There are, however, certain relationships between the frequencies of the formants and the sizes and shapes of the resonating cavities. Some of these relationships can be seen by comparing the diagrams of the vocal tract shown in figure 7.5 with the corresponding spectra.

In general all the formant frequencies depend on **three**

..tors: the position of the point of maximum constriction in ..1e vocal tract (which is controlled by the backward and forward movement of the tongue); the size or cross-sectional area of the maximum constriction (which is controlled by the movements of the tongue towards and away from the roof of the mouth and the back of the throat); and the position of the lips.

For vowels such as those in *heed, hid, head,* and *had,* the chief cause of the variation in the frequency of the first formant is the variation in the size of the maximum constriction in the vocal tract. The tongue is closest to the roof of the mouth for the word *heed;* and for each of the other words, it is a little less close. As a rough rule we can say that for vowels of this sort, as the cross-sectional area of the maximum constriction of the vocal tract increases, so the frequency of the lowest formant also increases. For vowels such as those in *hod, hawed, hood,* and *who'd* the variation in the frequency of the first formant is largely determined by the position of the point of maximum constriction. In these vowels the constriction is in the throat or the back of the mouth; and during this series it moves progressively forward. As the point of maximum constriction moves further from the glottis, the frequency of the first formant decreases.

The variation in the frequency of the second formant in the vowels in the words *heed, hid, head* and *had,* also depends mainly on the variation in the size of the maximum constriction in the vocal tract. But the rule is the reverse of that applicable to the first formant: as the constriction increases, so the frequency of the second formant decreases. But variations in the second formant are also due to the rounding of the lips. However, this movement will cause in addition a decrease in the relative sizes of the second and higher peaks. In the series of words *heed, hid, head, had, hod, hawed, hood, who'd,* the lips become progressively more rounded. In the last four of these words it is the movement of the lips rather than the movement of the tongue which results in the lowering of the frequency of the second resonance peak. Note that the increase in lip rounding also accounts for the decrease in the relative amplitudes of the second and third peaks in the last four words of the series.

Many other sounds of speech are formed in a similar way to the vowels which we have been describing. For example, nasal sounds, such as those at the ends of the words *him, sin,* and *sing,* and laterals, such as those at the beginnings and ends of the words *little* and *lull,* also depend on pulses from the vocal cords setting the air in the vocal tract in vibration. For each of these sounds there are characteristic positions of the vocal organs, and consequently a particular resonance curve can be associated with each of them. During the pronunciation of the first sound in the word *mat,* for instance, the vocal organs are in the positions shown in figure 7.10. The lips are closed but the air passage through the nose is open. This particular shape of the vocal tract has a resonance curve as shown in figure 7.11. The largest damped waves which are characteristic of this sound have basic frequencies of about 650 cps. and 2,500 cps.

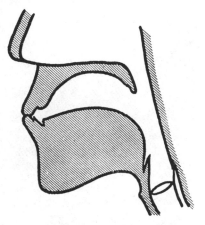

FIG. 7.10. The position of the vocal organs during the [m] in *mat.*

In the English vowels, nasals, and laterals, the main source of acoustic energy is the production of pulses by the vocal cords. But the stream of breath from the lungs can be used to form sounds in other ways. A typical speech sound in which the vocal cords are not in action occurs at the beginning of the word *sip.* When we say this word we begin by raising the tongue so that it is close behind the upper front teeth, forming a very narrow gap through which the air from the lungs is forced. As a result of this there are many small semi-random variations in air pressure which taken together constitute the high frequency hissing noise which we associate with the letter *s*. The relative amplitudes of the frequency components in this sound are largely determined by the shape of the narrow channel

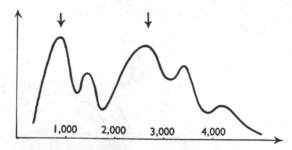

FIG. 7.11. The resonance curve of the vocal tract during the pronunciation of the first sound in the word *mat*.

made by the tongue; but the shape of the cavities in the throat and mouth will also have some effect on the component frequencies. If, for instance, you try slightly rounding your lips while saying an *s* sound, you will find that there is a drop in the apparent pitch of the sound. However, this effect is small in comparison with variations caused by alterations in the shape of the gap through which the air is forced. The general rule is that the smaller the gap the higher the apparent pitch of the sound. This may be verified by pronouncing the sounds [s, ʃ, θ, f] (as in *sin*, *shin*, *thin*, and *fin*). The very narrow channel at the beginning of the word *sin* produces a high frequency noise; a slightly broader channel results in the lower-pitched sound at the beginning of *shin*; the even broader channel between the tongue and the upper front teeth at the beginning of the word *thin* produces a still lower-pitched sound, and the very broad channel between the lower lip and the upper teeth which occurs at the beginning of the word *fin* produces a sound where most of the energy is distributed among even lower frequencies.

Some speech sounds are formed by a combination of the two mechanisms which we have discussed so far. Thus the sound at the beginning of the word *zoo,* for instance, is the result of setting the air in the vocal tract vibrating by means of pulses from the vocal cords, and at the same time generating additional variations in air pressure by forcing air through a narrow channel as in the production of an [s] sound. The sounds at the beginnings of the words *vat* and *that* are also formed by a combination of these two acoustic mechanisms.

One of the other sounds of English which it is interesting to discuss is the sound which is usually written with the letter *h.* In this sound the vocal cords are not in action as they are when we say a vowel; nor is there any acoustic energy generated by forcing air through a narrow gap. Instead the air from the lungs has a relatively free passage out through the vocal tract. But whenever an airstream passes through the vocal cavities some small variations in air pressure will be caused by the irregular surfaces which obstruct the flow; and these pressure variations will be sufficient to produce very slight vibrations of the body of air in the vocal tract. As the positions of the articulators during the sound [h] are the same as in the vowel which follows the [h], the frequency components in [h] sounds have similar relative amplitudes to those in vowels; but the complex wave has a smaller amplitude, and no fundamental frequency, since it is not generated by regular pulses from the vocal cords.

It may be useful to finish off this survey of some of the sounds of English with a brief account of the sounds at the beginnings and ends of the words *pip, bib, tit, did, kick,* and *gig.* Of course the consonants in these words should be thought of not as sounds in themselves but as ways of beginning and ending the vowels. Each of them involves an abrupt change in the wave form associated with the vowel.

The consonants in the words *pip*, *tit*, and *kick* are distinguished from those in *bib*, *did*, and *gig* by the action of the vocal cords. In the latter group the vocal cords begin generating pulses earlier in the articulation of each word and continue doing so for longer than in the first group. Within each group the words are partly distinguished from one another by differences in the shape of the vocal tract. During the word *gig*, for instance, the tongue is at no time in any of the positions that it passes through during the pronunciation of the word *did*. (If you want to check this try saying a sentence such as *Did he get his gig?* You will probably find that at no time during the first word is the tip of the tongue behind the lower front teeth, where it is throughout the last word; and during all the last word the back of the tongue is raised towards the soft palate, whereas in the first word it is relatively flat in the mouth.) These differences in the shape of the vocal tract affect the vowels in each of these words; and the shape of the vocal tract as it moves to or from a position for a consonant closure also results in the accompanying sounds having characteristic qualities. We associate these different qualities with the different consonants at the beginnings and ends of these words.

Many of the acoustic differences between speech sounds have not yet been fully investigated. Nearly all of them, however, can be described in terms of the general theories outlined in this book. It is hoped that a knowledge of these principles will enable the reader to appreciate some of the problems which are being discussed in contemporary papers on acoustic phonetics.

Glossary

Note: The explanations given in this glossary should be regarded not as definitions, but as general guides useful for the reader who is not specially trained in mathematics and physics.

AMPLITUDE. The increase (or decrease) of air pressure at a given point during a sound. In the wave form shown in figure G.1, the amplitude at time a is designated by the line a–a'.

> R.M.S. AMPLITUDE. A form of average of the amplitude especially useful when discussing complex wave forms. The r.m.s. amplitude (which is indirectly associated with the LOUDNESS of the sound) is indicated by a dashed line in figure G.1.

BANDWIDTH. The range of frequencies over which a resonator or a filter will respond effectively. The response to a uniform input is often considered to be effective within the frequency range where the output has an amplitude at least 70·7% (i.e. it has a power at least 50%) of the maximum output.

BASIC FREQUENCY. See under FREQUENCY.

COMPLEX WAVE. Any wave which is not a SINE WAVE.

COMPONENT. See under FREQUENCY COMPONENT.

CYCLE. When a wave form repeats itself a number of times each complete repetition is called a cycle. Thus a cycle is that part of the wave between any point (e.g. the point marked a in figure G.1) and the next point (that marked b) where the variations in air pressure start to go through precisely the same set of changes again.

DAMPING. Causing vibrations or variations in air pressure to die away. A highly damped sound (i.e. one which dies away quickly) has its energy spread over a wide range of component frequencies. Figure G.4 shows the wave form and figure G.5 shows the SPECTRUM of such a sound.

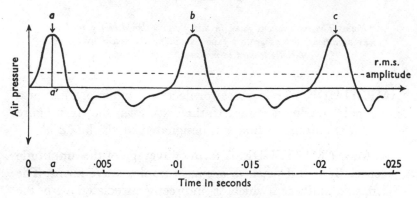

FIG. G.I. A complex wave.

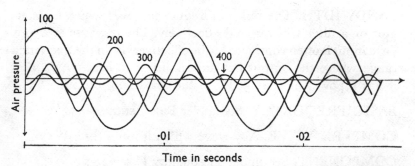

FIG. G.2. The component frequencies of the complex wave in fig. G.I.

DECIBEL. A useful measurement for comparing the POWER (and hence, roughly, the LOUDNESS) of two sounds. The difference in decibels between two sounds is equal to ten times the common logarithm of the power ratio of the two sounds.

FREQUENCY. The number of complete CYCLES occurring in a second. For instance, a tuning fork emitting a note of concert pitch *a* is making 440 complete back-and-forth movements per second; its frequency is therefore 440 cycles per second (cps.). The frequency of the complex wave shown in figure G.1 is 100 cps., since each cycle (e.g. from *a* to *b*) lasts 0·01 second, i.e. one-hundredth of a second. A variation in the frequency of a wave form is usually accompanied by a variation in the PITCH of the sound.

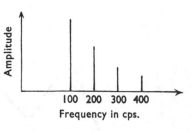

FIG. G.3. The spectrum of the complex wave in fig. G.1.

FREQUENCY COMPO-NENT. One of a number of SINE WAVES which can be considered as being present in a complex wave. If the wave shown in figure G.1 continued indefinitely we could say that it consisted of the four frequency components shown in figure G.2.

FUNDAMENTAL FREQUENCY. The frequency of repetition of a complex wave (i.e. 100 cps. in figure G.1). When a repetitive wave form is analysed into its component frequencies the fundamental is the highest common factor of the component frequencies. The component with this frequency (which is 100 cps. for the wave in figure G.2) may have a large amplitude, or (in analyses of other wave forms) it may have a small amplitude, or (as in the case of the wave in figure 6.3) there may not be any component with this frequency.

BASIC FREQUENCY. The most important frequency component, usually the one with the largest amplitude. The wave form shown in figure G.4 has a basic frequency of 1,000 cps. (As this is a non-repetitive form it cannot be said to have a FUNDAMENTAL FREQUENCY.)

HARMONIC. A whole-number multiple of the fundamental frequency of a wave form. If a complex wave form has a fundamental frequency of 200 cps., the components with frequencies of 400 cps. and 600 cps. are usually called the second and third harmonics. The sound described by figures G.1, G.2, and G.3 consists of the fundamental, the second, the third, and the fourth harmonics. All the other harmonics are missing.

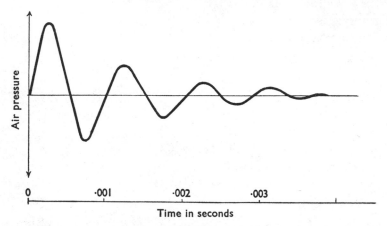

Fig. G.4. A damped wave.

LOUDNESS. The auditory property of a sound which enables a listener to place the sound on a scale going from soft to loud, without considering the acoustic (or physical) properties of the sound.

PITCH. The auditory property of a sound which enables a listener to place the sound on a scale going from low to high, without considering the acoustic (or physical) properties of the sound.

POWER. The power of a sound is proportional to the square of the R.M.S. AMPLITUDE. Thus if the r.m.s. amplitude of a sound is trebled, the power is increased by a factor of three squared, i.e. by nine.

RESONANCE. The phenomenon whereby one body, which has a natural tendency to vibrate at a certain frequency, will build up vibrations with a comparatively large amplitude when it is set in motion by another body which is vibrating at a similar frequency. The amplitude of the forced vibrations will increase as the frequency of the driving system more nearly approaches the natural frequency of the resonator.

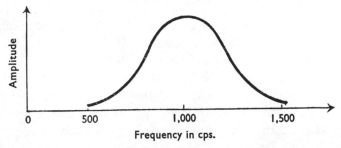

FIG. G.5. The spectrum of the non-repetitive wave form shown in fig. G.4.

RESONANCE CURVE. An indication of the relative amplitudes of the vibrations which would be made by a body in response to different driving frequencies. Thus figure G.6 is the resonance curve of a body (which might

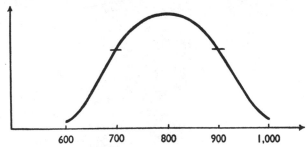

FIG. G.6. A curve specifying a resonator.

well be a body of air contained in a tube something like the vocal tract) which would respond best to a tone of 800 cps., and would respond only half as well to frequencies of 700 and 900 cps. When a body responds to a wide range of frequencies it is said to be a DAMPED resonator.

SINE WAVE. One of the simplest kinds of regular variation (in air pressure). A pure tone has a wave form with the shape of a sine wave.

SINUSOIDAL. Having the shape of a sine wave.

SPECTRUM. A diagram showing the relative amplitudes of the frequency components of a sound. If the wave form shown in figure G.1 continued indefinitely, the sound would have only four components, and the spectrum would be a LINE SPECTRUM (one line for each component) as shown in figure G.3. A non-repetitive wave form such as the damped wave in figure G.4 has an infinite number of components in its spectrum which is as shown in figure G.5. This type of spectrum is called a continuous spectrum.

WHITE NOISE. A sound with an equal amount of power at every component frequency over the audible range.

Annotated Bibliography

Note: This bibliography was revised in 1971.

There are two classic books which should be read by all students of acoustic phonetics:

1. M. Joos, *Acoustic Phonetics* (LANGUAGE, Monograph No. 23, Supplement to LANGUAGE, Vol. 24, No. 2, 1948).

2. R. K. Potter, G. Kopp, and H. Green, *Visible Speech* (New York, 1947).

The first of these two books begins with a condensed treatment of most of the same topics as the present book, and then goes on to develop a fairly elaborate treatment of the linguistic implications of acoustic data. Fortunately the speculative discussions are plainly labelled as speculative, so that it is possible to correct them where necessary.

The second (earlier) book is rather journalistic and directed towards commercial applications, especially in the service of the deaf. It contains a good deal of useful material mixed with misleading things; its treatment of isolated sounds is particularly dangerous because of the artificiality of the sounds taken as samples (e.g., clear and steady "English" vowels instead of the normal obscure and diphthongized ones, etc.). Correction of this book is more difficult, so that it needs to be read with great caution.

Much of the other relevant material is contained in journals (especially in the *Journal of the Acoustical Society of America*). Several papers from this journal and others have been collected in:

3. Ilse Lehiste, ed., *Readings in Acoustic Phonetics* (Cambridge, Mass.: M.I.T. Press, 1967).

The most authoritative account of the acoustics of speech is still:

4. G. Fant, *Acoustic Theory of Speech Production* (The Hague: Mouton, 1960).

This book is undoubtedly the leading work in the field. There is a fair amount of detailed mathematical specification of the acoustic properties of the vocal tract, but much of the book can be read with profit by all students of speech.

Fant has written many other books and articles, some of which are included in reference 3 above. His most comprehensive review of the field of acoustic phonetics is in:

5. B. Malmberg, ed., *Manual of Phonetics* (Amsterdam: North-Holland, 1968).

This book also contains a number of other excellent articles on experimental phonetics.

The best introductory book containing material on acoustic phonetics is:

6. P. B. Denes and E. N. Pinson, *The Speech Chain: The Physics and Biology of Spoken Language* (Bell Telephone Laboratories, 1963).

Other relevant books (listed in alphabetical order) include:

7. W. A. van Bergeijk, J. R. Pierce, and E. E. David, *Waves and the Ear* (London: Heinemann, 1961).

A good elementary account of the physical nature of sound and the physiology of the ear.

8. R. Chiba and M. Kajiyama, *The Vowel: Its Nature and Structure* (Tokyo: Phonetic Society of Japan, 1941; reprinted by offset lithography with new title page and typographical errors corrected 1958).

Despite its age, this book remains a major source for acoustic and physiological data on vowels.

9. G. Fant, "Acoustic Analysis and Synthesis of Speech, with Application to Swedish" (*Ericson Technics*, vol. 1, 1959; reprinted 1969).

The work is fairly technical, but contains a great deal of useful data.

10. J. L. Flanagan, *Speech Analysis, Synthesis and Perception* (New York: Academic Press, 1965) . ;

A technical review of recent work written largely from an engineer's point of view.

11. H. L. F. Helmholtz, *Sensations of Tone*, translated by A. J. Ellis (New York: Dover Publications, 2d ed., 1885, reprinted 1954) .

Of great importance for anyone interested in the history of phonetics; the translation—by one of the leading phoneticians of the time—has numerous additional notes and appendices.

12. Peter Ladefoged, *Three Areas of Experimental Phonetics* (London: Oxford University Press, 1967) .

A consolidated account of earlier work, including a long section on auditory and acoustic parameters of vowel quality.

13. Peter Ladefoged, *A Phonetic Study of West African Languages* (Cambridge: Cambridge University Press, 1964) .

Includes examples of the use of a wide range of instrumental techniques as an aid in making linguistic descriptions.

14. Ilse Lehiste, *Suprasegmentals* (Cambridge, Mass.: M.I.T. Press, 1970) .

This book provides several excellent examples of the use of acoustic phonetic techniques for collecting linguistically relevant data.

Index

Amplitude: 15, 109
articulatory—acoustic correlates: 103
auditory area: 85

Bandwidth: 65, 69, 84, 109
basic frequency: 72, 111
bib: 107

Caught: 25, 90 et seq.
complex wave: 109
components: 36, 111
continuous spectrum: 48
cycle: 19, 109

Damped resonators: 60
damping: 60, 88
db: 82
decibel: 82, 110
did: 107

Ear: 1

f: 106
filter: 69
fin: 106
fish: 32
formant: 92
Fourier analysis: 34
frequency: 19, 111
fundamental frequency: 36, 111

gig: 107

h: 107
had: 96 et seq., 101 et seq.
half power bandwidth: 84
harmonic: 36, 112
hawed: 96 et seq., 101 et seq.
head: 96 et seq., 101 et seq.
heed: 96 et seq., 101 et seq.

hid: 96 et seq., 101 et seq.
him: 105
hiss: 29, 32, 53, 54
hod: 96 et seq., 101 et seq.
hood: 96 et seq., 101 et seq.
hush: 53, 54

Joos: 99, 105

Kick: 107
Koenig scale: 77

Laterals: 105
limits of hearing: 85
line spectrum: 48
loudness: 13, 14, 79, 112

Masking: 86
mat: 105
mel scale: 77

Nasal sounds: 105
non-repetitive wave form: 30

Octave: 20

Pat: 48
peak: 31
phase: 39
pip: 107
pitch: 13, 17, 71, 112
pitch scale: 76
power: 80, 112
power ratio: 81

Quality: 13, 22

Reference level: 81
resonance: 56, 113
resonance curve: 61, 113

resonant frequency: 65
r.m.s. amplitude: 79, 109

s: 106
see: 25, 41, 90 et seq.
shin: 106
sin: 105, 106
sine wave: 22, 113
sing: 105
sip: 105
sound spectrograph: 101
spectrum: 37, 113
∫: 106

That: 107
thin: 106
time constant: 67

tit: 107
transient: 33
θ: 106

Vat: 107
vocal cords: 89, 92, 95
vocal tract: 89
vowels: 90

Wave: 5
whispering: 103
white noise: 32, 114
who: 25
who'd: 96 et seq., 101 et seq.

Zoo: 107